Excel

YEARS 7 to 8

Writing and Spelling Workbook

ESSENTIAL skills

Get the Results You Want!

Bianca Hewes

Reprinted 2017, 2019, 2021, 2022, 2024

ISBN 978 1 74125 414 3

Pascal Press
PO Box 250
Glebe NSW 2037
(02) 9198 1748
www.pascalpress.com.au

Publisher: Vivienne Joannou
Series developer and consultant: Kristine Brown
Project editors: Mark Dixon and Leanne Poll
Edited by Leanne Howard
Reviewed by Justine Hodgson
Typeset by Grizzly Graphics (Leanne Richters)
Cover and page design by DiZign Pty Ltd
Printed by Vivar Printing/Green Giant Press

Contents

Informative texts

Imaginative texts

To the student

This book is designed to help you master the main language features and structures of some very common types of texts that you will encounter in school and in your life. Each chapter is designed to guide you through the process of planning, drafting and then writing a specific type of text. Take your time when completing the activities in each chapter as these will help you compose a stronger piece of writing at the end.

Each text will be persuasive, informative or imaginative. The Marking criteria section (pages viii–ix) outlines the features of advanced, intermediate and basic levels of writing. It's a good idea to read these criteria carefully so that you know what features are expected in a high-quality response.

Each chapter is divided into six sections. The exercises and examples in each chapter relate directly to the type of text that you are being asked to write.

- ***Understanding the question****—each chapter opens with a question asking you to write a specific type of text. This section gets you thinking about the type of question you have been asked. You will complete a couple of small activities about the chapter question.*
- ***Planning and organisation****—this section will help you plan the content for your piece of writing.*
- ***Structure****—this section will focus on the specific structure required for the type of text you have been asked to write.*
- ***Language feature****—this section focuses on the main language feature you will need to know and master for the type of text you have been asked to write.*
- ***Spotlight on spelling****—this section will give you the opportunity to identify spelling rules for yourself to help develop your spelling skills.*
- ***You be the teacher****—in this section you will look at a paragraph of a student's writing and make corrections based on the structure and spelling rules you have mastered in earlier sections of this chapter.*
- ***Now you write****—it is now time for you to put into practice everything you have just learned about this specific text type. You will now write your answer to the chapter question using the required type of text.*
- ***Looking at other students' writing****—you are given two examples of students' writing to look at closely. One is an advanced piece of writing and one is an intermediate piece of writing. Both are annotated to help you see the strengths and weaknesses of the students' writing and help guide you with your own writing.*

By the end of each chapter, you will have composed a complete and extended piece of writing. Writing should be an enjoyable and creative process, so I hope you enjoy this book!

Bianca Hewes

Marking criteria

Persuasive texts

Criteria	Advanced	Intermediate	Basic
Content: appropriateness to audience	• The text skilfully engages and persuades the audience. • The text uses an excellent selection and elaboration of ideas relevant to the persuasive text topic. • A wide variety of persuasive devices (such as rhetorical questions, repetition, strong verbs and adverbs) have been used to enhance the writer's position and persuade the audience to accept this position.	• The text engages and persuades the audience reasonably well. • There is sound selection and some elaboration of ideas relevant to the persuasive text topic. • Attempts have been made to use persuasive devices (such as rhetorical questions, repetition, high modal adverbs) to enhance the writer's position and persuade the audience to accept this position.	• The text fails to engage and persuade the audience. • The writing shows a weak selection and minimal elaboration of ideas relevant to the persuasive text topic. • Few persuasive devices have been used.
Mechanics: punctuation, spelling, sentence structure, vocabulary	• A wide range of precise and appropriate language choices have been made—specifically vocabulary relevant to the text topic. • All sentences are grammatically correct, structurally sound and meaningful. • All punctuation is correct. • All words are spelt correctly, including more complex and technical spelling words.	• Language choices are appropriate to the text topic but lack detail. • Most sentences are grammatically correct, structurally sound and meaningful. • Most punctuation is correct but there are some errors. • Most words are spelt correctly but there are some errors.	• Language choices may be inappropriate and not relevant to the text topic. • Sentences are unclear and contain obvious grammatical errors. • There are frequent punctuation errors. • There are frequent spelling errors and vocabulary is basic.
Form: text structure, paragraphing, cohesion	• The text has a highly effective structure appropriate to a persuasive text including an introduction, body and conclusion. • Connectives (e.g. *also*, *similarly*, *furthermore*) are used effectively for smooth and coherent transition between the main points in the text. • Highly effective division of the persuasive text into paragraphs is used to help the audience to follow the line of argument.	• Appropriate structure for a persuasive text is used, including introduction, body and conclusion, but may be disorganised or too short. • Attempts have been made to use connectives (e.g. *also*, *similarly*, *furthermore*) for smooth and coherent transition between the main points in the text. • The text is divided into paragraphs that help the audience to follow the line of argument.	• The speech is missing some or all of the required structural components. • Connectives (e.g. *also*, *similarly*, *furthermore*) are not used or are used inappropriately. • The text is not divided into paragraphs or the paragraphs are infrequent.

Informative texts

Criteria	Advanced	Intermediate	Basic
Content: appropriateness to audience	• The text skilfully engages and informs the audience. • The text uses an excellent selection and elaboration of ideas relevant to the informative text. • A wide variety of informative devices (such as objective language, headings, topic sentences, definitions, supporting evidence and factual tone) have been used to explain the topic of the informative text.	• The text engages and informs the audience reasonably well. • There is sound selection and some elaboration of ideas relevant to the informative text topic. • Attempts have been made to use informative devices (such as objective language, headings, topic sentences, definitions, supporting evidence and factual tone) to explain the topic of the informative text.	• The text fails to engage and inform the audience. • The writing shows a weak selection and minimal elaboration of ideas relevant to the informative text. • Few informative devices have been used.
Mechanics: punctuation, spelling, sentence structure, vocabulary	• A wide range of precise and appropriate language choices have been made—specifically vocabulary relevant to the topic. • All sentences are grammatically correct, structurally sound and meaningful. • All punctuation is correct. • All words are spelt correctly, including more complex and technical spelling words.	• Language choices are appropriate to the topic but lack detail. • Most sentences are grammatically correct, structurally sound and meaningful. • Most punctuation is correct but there are some errors. • Most words are spelt correctly but there are some errors.	• Language choices may be inappropriate and not relevant to the topic. • Sentences are unclear and contain obvious grammatical errors. • There are frequent punctuation errors. • There are frequent spelling errors and the vocabulary used is basic.
Form: text structure, paragraphing, cohesion	• The text has a highly effective structure appropriate to the informative type of text. • Connectives and conjunctions (e.g. *also*, *similarly*, *furthermore*) are used effectively for smooth and coherent transition between the main parts of the informative text. • Highly effective division of the informative text into paragraphs is used to help the audience to follow the key pieces of information.	• Structure appropriate to the informative type of text is used but may be disorganised or too short. • Attempts have been made to use connectives and conjunctions (e.g. *also*, *similarly*, *furthermore*) for smooth and coherent transition between the main points in the speech. • The text is divided into paragraphs that help the audience to follow the key pieces of information.	• The text is missing some or all of the required structural components. • Connectives and conjunctions (e.g. *also*, *similarly*, *furthermore*) are not used or are used inappropriately. • The text is not divided into paragraphs or the paragraphs are infrequent.

Imaginative texts

Criteria	Advanced	Intermediate	Basic
Content: audience, narrative devices, ideas	• The text skilfully engages the audience in experiences, events or characters. • There is excellent development of real or imagined experiences or events using relevant descriptive details. • A wide variety of narrative devices (such as dialogue, description, figurative language and mood) have been used to develop experiences, events, and/or characters.	• The text engages the audience reasonably well in experiences, events or characters. • There is sound development of real or imagined experiences or events using relevant descriptive details. • Attempts have been made to use narrative devices (such as dialogue, description, figurative language and mood) to develop experiences, events and/or characters.	• The text fails to engage the audience. • There is weak development of real or imagined experiences or events using relevant descriptive details. • Few narrative devices have been used.
Mechanics: punctuation, spelling, sentence structure, vocabulary	• A wide range of precise and appropriate language choices have been made—specifically descriptive details, and sensory language relevant to the topic. • All sentences are grammatically correct, structurally sound and meaningful. • All punctuation is correct. • All words are spelt correctly, including more complex and challenging spelling words.	• Language choices are appropriate to the topic but lack detail. • Most sentences are grammatically correct, structurally sound and meaningful. • Most punctuation is correct but there are some errors. • Most words are spelt correctly but there are some errors.	• Language choices may be inappropriate and not relevant to the topic. • Sentences are unclear and contain obvious grammatical errors. • There are frequent punctuation errors. • There are frequent spelling errors and vocabulary is basic.
Form: text structure, paragraphing, cohesion	• Highly effective structure appropriate to the narrative type of text has been used. • A variety of transition words, phrases, and/or clauses convey sequence and signal shifts from one time frame or setting to another. • Highly effective division of the text into paragraphs that helps the audience to follow the key elements of the narrative.	• Appropriate structure for the narrative type of text is used but may be disorganised or too short. • A variety of transition words, phrases, and/or clauses are used to convey sequence and signal shifts from one time frame or setting to another. • The text is segmented into paragraphs that help the audience follow the key elements of the narrative.	• The text is missing some or all of the required structural components. • The text uses few, if any, transition words, phrases, and/or clauses to convey sequence and signal shifts from one time frame or setting to another. • The text is not divided into paragraphs or the paragraphs are infrequent.

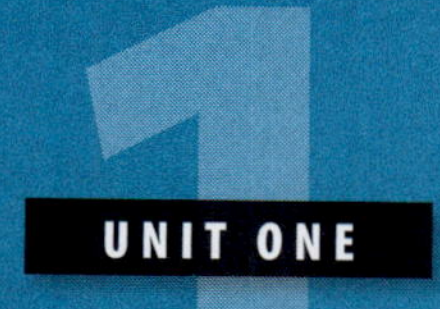

Persuasive texts

Persuasive speeches

Understanding the question

Write a speech addressing the question below:
Should fireworks be banned for personal use in Australia?

Type of question

This question is asking you to write a particular type of speech—a **persuasive speech**.

How do you know it is a persuasive speech wanted and not an informative speech? The word *should* is the best clue. It shows you are required to **adopt a position** on the topic—a point of view. Here you are being asked to adopt a position arguing **for** or **against** the banning of fireworks for personal use in Australia.

Features of a persuasive speech

- Aims to influence or convince the audience to agree with the speaker
- Argues for or against a particular issue
- Often aims to influence the way the audience thinks and behaves
- Provides arguments to support a particular point of view
- Supports ideas with evidence
- Has a broad structure: introduction, body and conclusion
- Uses persuasive language
- Should be highly engaging

Every question contains important '**content words**'. These words help you work out what should be discussed in your answer and what you should keep your focus on. Look again at the question above. It includes four key content words that tell you what you must focus on in your speech.

fireworks   banned   Australia   personal use

Content words
These are the main verbs and nouns that tell you what you need to discuss in your response to the question.

1 Write a brief definition of each of the **content words** below. You might want to use a dictionary to help you.

a fireworks ______________________________

____

b banned ______________________________

____

c personal use ______________________________

____

Planning and organisation

You must **plan** before every piece of writing you do.

Planning is important because it helps you:

* **develop and organise your ideas** in response to the question
* ensure you are **keeping to the task** and type of text.

Activity 1

On the spider-map below, add all you know about the **speech topic**. Be sure to focus on reasons **for** and **against** the banning of fireworks for personal use in Australia.

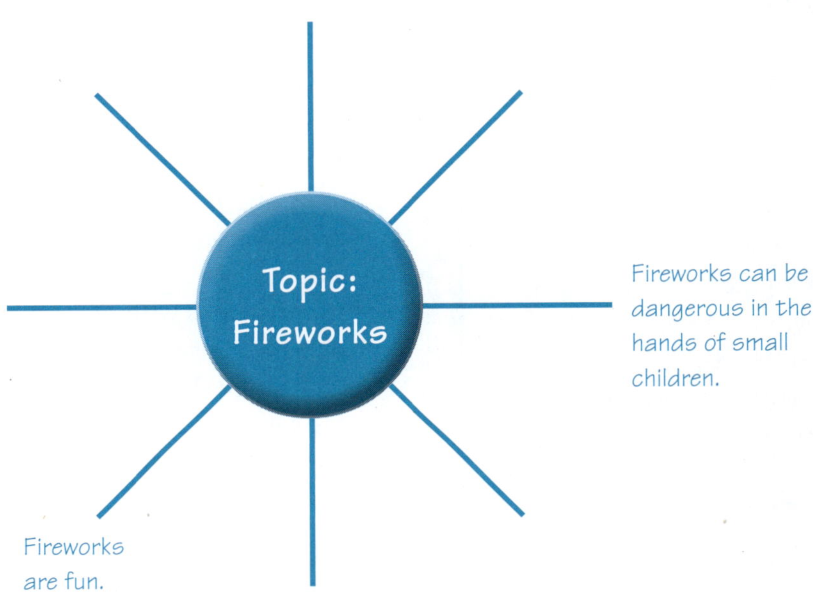

Activity 2

Using the information from the spider-map above, complete the following **for** and **against** table.

Question: Should fireworks be banned for personal use in Australia?	
For	**Against**

Activity 3

Looking at the information on the previous page, now think about which side you agree with most strongly—in other words, decide your **position** on the topic. Your position will have you either stating that you are **for** or **against** fireworks being banned for personal use in Australia. Use the following mind-map to expand your argument—you will need to include your position, your reasons for adopting this position, as well as evidence to support your position.

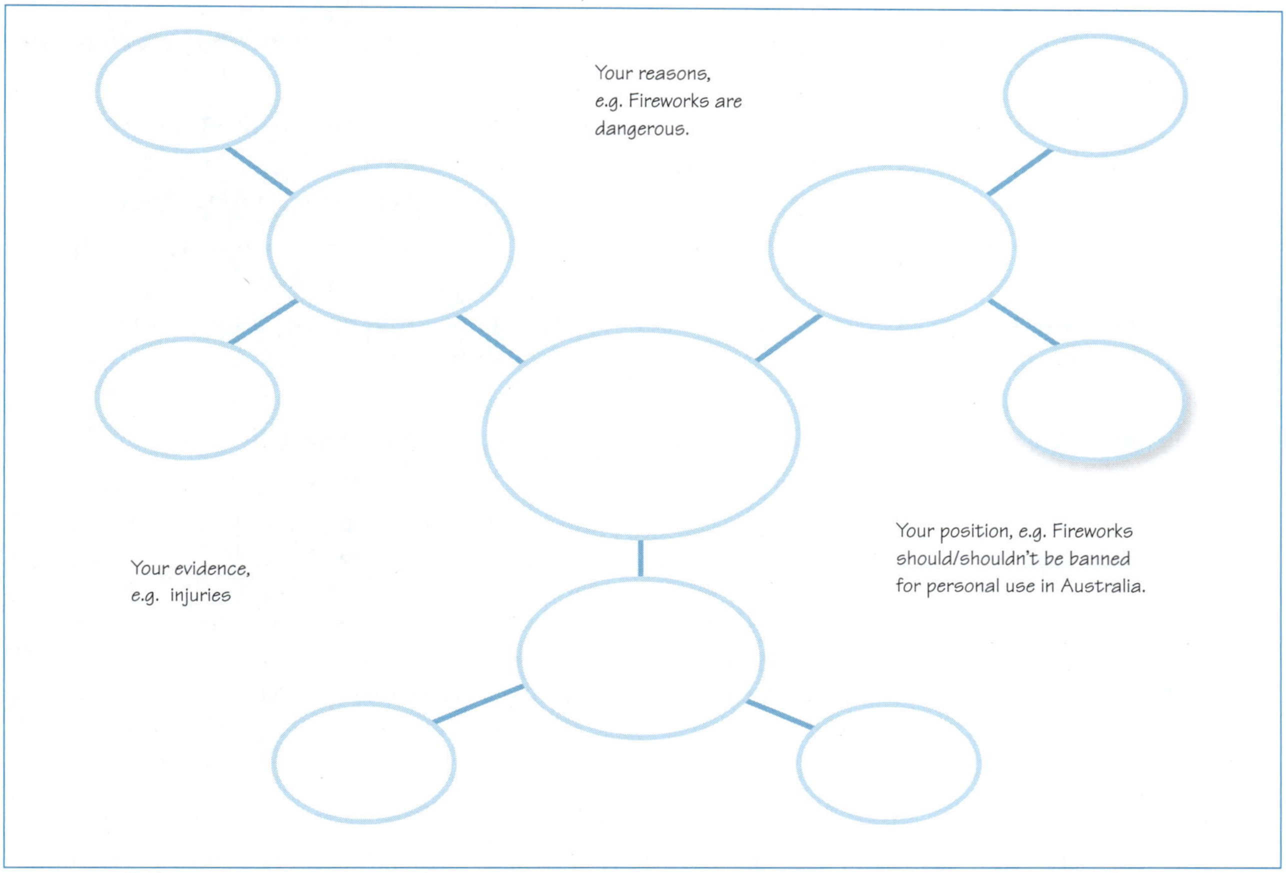

Your reasons, e.g. Fireworks are dangerous.

Your position, e.g. Fireworks should/shouldn't be banned for personal use in Australia.

Your evidence, e.g. injuries

A good persuasive speech will feature no less than THREE main reasons why the speaker holds a specific position. You should also provide at least ONE piece of evidence to support each of your reasons.

Structure

The last few activities were designed to get you thinking and planning. Now you're going to complete some activities to help you learn about the structure and language features of a **persuasive speech**.

The **structure** of a persuasive speech is the same as the structure of an informative speech with three main parts: **introductory** paragraph, **body** paragraphs and **concluding** paragraph. The difference between the persuasive and informative speech is the type of language used. Persuasive speeches **use language to persuade**.

Introductory paragraph

In this paragraph you need to **grab the attention** of your audience and **outline** the topic you will be speaking about.

* **Greet your audience.** You should mention special guests in the audience by name and greet the group as a whole. For example: 'Good morning Ms Woods, Mr Moran and my fellow Year 7 students.'
* You then need an 'attention grabber'. There are four possible ways to **grab the attention** of your audience.
    * **Tell a joke**—if you love making people laugh, here's your chance, just make sure your joke relates to your speech topic!
    * **Ask a rhetorical question**—this is a type of question where you don't expect an answer. Your question must link to your topic and encourage your audience to reflect on what you are asking them.
    * **State a statistic about your topic**—this should be used for maximum impact on your audience. It's important that this is an actual statistic, not one that you have made up.
    * **Make a strong statement**—this should be dramatic and show your position about your chosen topic.
* The remaining two or three sentences of your opening paragraph should further establish the topic of your speech and, most importantly, your position on this topic.

Some attention grabbers may not be appropriate for your speech topic. For example, telling a joke might not be a good idea for a serious speech.

Activity 1

Match each type of **attention grabber** with its correct example. The first one has been done for you.

a statistic	Why didn't the chicken cross the road? Because it was afraid of the fireworks.
b rhetorical question	There's no use denying it, the end of the world is coming.
c joke	Infant mortality for Indigenous Australians is three times that of other Australians.
d statement	When was the last time you thought about the feelings of the animal on the end of your fork?

Activity 2

It is now time for you to draft the **introduction** to your persuasive speech on the following topic: *Should fireworks be banned for personal use in Australia?*

Remember to begin with an attention grabber!

Body paragraphs

Each **body paragraph** will deal with one, and only one, reason why you hold your position. For example, your first paragraph might focus on your opinion that fireworks should be banned because they are dangerous.

For a persuasive speech we use the **SEW paragraph structure**.

Statement: Open each new paragraph with a strong and clear statement on one of the three reasons for your position (already identified during the planning stage). Provide further detail about this statement in your second sentence.

Evidence or example: In one or two sentences, provide evidence or an example to support this statement. The evidence you use can vary widely from a statistic to the description of a personal experience.

Why: Explain why this reason and evidence support the position you have adopted on the speech topic.

Between each body paragraph you should use **connectives** to show links between your ideas. Some connectives you might use include *furthermore, in addition, moreover, also, however* and *similarly*. You can find out more about connectives in Unit 2.

Activity 3

In the following example of a good body paragraph:

a highlight the **Statement**
b underline the **Evidence**
c put a circle around the **Why**.

Removing meat from your diet can not only save you, but it could save the world. Did you know that in the United States approximately 41 million tonnes of plant protein is fed to livestock each year? Growing this plant protein requires large amounts of water and energy—things our world has in short supply. To protect the health of our planet it is clear that we must stop eating meat.

Activity 4

Go back to the notes you made during the planning stage. Use these to draft **one body paragraph** for your persuasive speech. Remember to use the SEW structure!

Concluding paragraph

The concluding paragraph of your speech is important because it has the final impact on your audience.

A **concluding paragraph** has four elements. It:

- **signals** the end of your talk
- **summarises** your main points
- **suggests** a call to action or **provides** a memorable statement or quotation
- **thanks** your audience for listening.

Activity 5

Draft the **concluding paragraph** for your speech, checking that you have included all four of these elements.

____

____

____

____

____

____

Language feature

Modality

You're so very close to putting pen to paper and writing your complete persuasive speech! Before that, however, we will look at one very important language feature of persuasive speeches—modality.

Modality refers to our use of certain words and phrases to show how certain we feel about an idea or how **strongly** we view it. These words and phrases are very useful when writing a persuasive text.

> **Modal verbs**
> We use these to show our attitude to what we are talking or writing about:
> *can, could, may, might, must, ought to, shall, should, will* and *would.*

We can show that **we are certain** or **feel strongly** about an idea by using, for example:

obviously always definitely never clearly undoubtedly absolutely

We can show that **we are uncertain** or **feel less strongly** about an idea by using, for example:

maybe possibly hopefully to an extent by chance sometimes perhaps

Activity 1

Select whether the underlined modals show **certainty or uncertainty** on the topic. The first one has been done for you.

- **a** Fireworks must remain banned as they are dangerous. CERTAIN / UNCERTAIN
- **b** Hopefully fireworks will become legal again one day. CERTAIN / UNCERTAIN
- **c** It is absolutely essential that adults supervise children with fireworks. CERTAIN / UNCERTAIN
- **d** It might be a good idea to let people use fireworks for their own entertainment. CERTAIN / UNCERTAIN
- **e** Maybe it would help if the authorities asked the citizens of Australia what they think about the issue. CERTAIN/UNCERTAIN

Activity 2

Circle the words and phrases that indicate the level of **certainty** or **uncertainty** in the sentences below.

a The government might want to give people permission to set off fireworks in their own backyard once a year.

b People must be careful when lighting fireworks.

c Perhaps if there were better rules for personal firework usage then a ban could be lifted.

d Fireworks should absolutely never be used near children or the elderly.

Activity 3

Change the sentences below from **certain** to **uncertain** by altering the modal used. There is more than one way to do this.

a Australian politicians must not allow fireworks to be legalised for personal use.

____

____

____

b Fireworks should be sold with a warning label.

____

____

____

Activity 4

Look back now at your draft introduction, body paragraph and conclusion, and underline any **language** you have used to show how **certain** or **strongly** you feel about your ideas. If you have not used any such language, make any changes you think are needed.

Spotlight *on spelling*

Adverbs

When writing a persuasive speech you will find you need to use **adverbs** to modify nouns and adjectives. Why? Because saying that it is a *horribly cruel industry* is **more persuasive** than simply saying it is a *cruel industry*. Spelling adverbs can be tricky as you are often required to add the suffix *ly* to a root word, typically an adjective.

What is a suffix?

Suffixes stand **after** a root word. There are many different types of suffixes: they can change both the spelling and meaning of the root word. For example: quick**ly**, dark**ness**, hope**ful** and terror**ism**.

Normally to create an adverb you simply add the suffix *ly* without altering the root word.

For example: strong + *ly* → strong**ly**

Activity 1

Turn the following adjectives into **adverbs**.

Adjective	Adverb
a certain	______________________
b definite	______________________
c hopeful	______________________
d frequent	______________________
e entire	______________________

For adjectives ending in *le* you must drop the *e* before you add *ly*.

For example: feeb**le** → feeb**ly**

Activity 2

Turn the following adjectives into **adverbs**.

Adjective	Adverb
a possible	______________________
b responsible	______________________
c arguable	______________________
d abominable	______________________
e able	______________________

For adjectives ending in *y*, drop the *y* and add *ily*.

For example: pretty → prett**ily**

Activity 3

Turn the following adjectives into **adverbs**.

Adjective	Adverb
a ordinary	______________________
b happy	______________________
c angry	______________________
d compulsory	______________________
e derogatory	______________________

You be the teacher

Below is a **body paragraph** for a persuasive speech written by a Year 7 student. There are some errors in the structure of the paragraph and the spelling of some of the adverbs. Rewrite the paragraph with the **correct SEW structure** and with the **correct spelling of all adverbs**.

This is one reasson why I believe fireworks must be permitted for personal use in Australia. One reason that fireworks definitlly shouldn't be banned in Australia is because they provide parents with an opportunity to teach children valuable lessons about explosives. Fireworks are amazingely beautiful however they can be dangerous if children attempt to use them without parental guidance. Clearlly the beauty of fireworks brings families together in a learning experience. When was the last time you looked up in the evening sky to discover brilliant colours and shapes?

Now you write

It is now time for you to complete your own **persuasive speech** on the fireworks topic.

1. Before you write, take some time to look at the student writing samples on the following pages as a guide to writing standards. Note the mistakes made in the Intermediate sample and try to avoid making these mistakes yourself.

2. Once you have read the two student writing samples, take some time to think about what you believe are the most important features of a persuasive speech that you need to master. Use the lines below to jot down your answer to this question:

   What do you find most difficult when writing this kind of text?

3. Now look at the persuasive text marking criteria on page vii to double-check that you understand the requirements for a really good piece of persuasive writing.

   Remember that you have already done your planning and drafted your introductory paragraph, one body paragraph and concluding paragraph. Use your own paper. Good luck!

Looking at other students' writing

Write a persuasive speech addressing the question below:
Should we stop eating animals?

ADVANCED SAMPLE

SHOULD WE STOP EATING ANIMALS?

When was the last time you thought about the feelings of the animal on the end of your fork? More often than not people do not stop to consider the life that was sacrificed for the food on their plates. People should immediately stop eating meat. Why? The killing of animals for food brings with it untold cruelty. If you are not concerned for the welfare of animals, think about yourselves. A meat-free diet is far healthier for individuals and the health of the world.

Animals are sentient beings capable of feeling pain, fear and loneliness. Should we still be seeing them as products? Today we are removed from the reality of meat, as we simply purchase it pre-packed at supermarkets. However, documentaries such as 'Food Inc' have revealed that the certain parts of the livestock industry allow cows, pigs and chickens to live in appalling conditions before they are slaughtered. This mistreatment of animals is highly unacceptable and therefore I believe we should stop eating animals.

Furthermore, eating a meat-free diet is a much healthier option. We all want to live a long life free from illness, right? A vegetarian diet provides individuals with all the nutrients a healthy body needs while eliminating the saturated fat found in meat. A diet high in saturated fat contributes to heart disease. Choosing to reduce or remove meat from your diet can make you a much healthier person.

Finally, removing meat from your diet can not only save you, but it could save the world. Did you know that in the United States approximately 41 million tonnes of plant protein is fed to livestock each year? Growing this plant protein requires large amounts of water and energy—things our world has in short supply. To protect the health of our planet it is clear that we definitely must stop eating meat.

To conclude I would like to summarise the main reasons why I believe we should stop eating animals. Animals have feelings and therefore deserve to be treated with kindness, not cruelty. Eating meat is not only bad for individuals, but it is bad for the future of our planet. So, in the interest of the animals, yourself and the world, I urge you to consider removing meat from your diet, if only for one day a week.

Thank you for listening.

Introduction
The introduction alerts the audience to the student's position —people should stop eating meat.

A rhetorical question engages the audience.

Persuasive techniques
The student uses many modal words to show certainty and enforce point of view. The student uses the collective first person *we* to persuade the audience that they feel the same way. Emotive words reinforce the speaker's position. The 'rule of three' is used—the three related words 'pain, fear and loneliness' grabs the audience's attention and creates sympathy.

Text structure
The student uses the correct structure of a speech, including an introduction, supporting paragraphs and conclusion.

Paragraphing
Each paragraph features one basic reason to support the author's point of view and evidence to support this reason. The student effectively uses the SEW paragraph structure. The conclusion is strong and includes all required elements.

Vocabulary
The student's language choices are appropriate to the purpose—to persuade people to stop eating meat. There is use of complex and precise words to talk about the topic.

Sentence structure
All sentences are grammatically correct, well structured and meaningful. The student uses a variety of sentence patterns.

Ideas
The ideas are well selected and relevant, with a lot of detail to support the speaker's position—we should stop eating animals.

Cohesion
The student uses connecting words to show clear connections between ideas, especially between reasons and evidence (e.g. *furthermore*).

Punctuation
Correct punctuation is used throughout the argument.

Spelling
All words are spelt correctly.

Write a persuasive speech addressing the question below: *Should we stop eating animals?*

Introduction
The student alerts the audience to the author's position in the first sentence and summarises this position. The student needs to grab the audience's attention more effectively with a rhetorical question or strong statement.

Sentence structure
The student uses a variety of simple and compound sentences. but needs to include more complex sentences that demonstrate a better control of language.

INTERMEDIATE SAMPLE

SHOULD WE STOP EATING ANIMALS?

I don't like it how people don't stop 2 consider the animal that died to be food on their plates. People should stop eating meat. The killing of animals for food is mean. If you don't care about the happiness of animals, think about yourselves. A meat-free diet is better for individuales and the health of the world.

Animals can feel pain and fear and we should stop eating them. Today we don't know where our meat comes from—we just buy it at the shop's. Shows like 'Food Inc' show that cows, pigs and chickens live in bad conditions before they are killed. This cruelness of animals is bad and I think we should stop eating animals.

Eating a meat-free diet is a much healthiar option. A diet with lots of fat leads to heart disease.

Removing meat from your diet could save the world. Did you know that in the US heaps of grain is fed to animals each year? Growing these needs lots of water and energy—things our world hasn't got much of. We haven't got much of these but. To protect our planet we must stop eating meat.

The main reasons I believe we should stop eating animals are animals have feelings and should be treated with kindness, not cruelty. eating meat is not only bad for individuals' but it is bad for the future of our planet. So, I think you should stop eating meat?

Ideas
The student uses good ideas that are relevant to the argument. Their ideas need more detail as they are quite general.

Persuasive techniques
The student uses some modal verbs and adverbs to show certainty and uses some emotive words, in this case to create sympathy for animals.

The emotive words used need to be less simplistic and more precise (e.g. *bad* could be *appalling*).

Punctuation
Simple punctuation is mostly used correctly, apart from some errors in punctuation (e.g. missing capital letter and incorrect use of possessive apostrophe).

Paragraphing
Each paragraph features one basic reason to support the point of view.

The paragraphs need to give more detail to support the student's ideas, especially paragraph three.

Cohesion
The student uses basic connectives to show connections between paragraphs (*and* and *so*) but needs to use many more connectives to link up ideas so it's easier for listeners to follow.

Text structure
The student uses the correct structure of a persuasive text including an introduction, supporting paragraphs and a conclusion. The student needs to thank the audience for listening.

Vocabulary
The language used is mostly appropriate to the student's purpose. More complex and exact vocabulary is needed (e.g. *supermarkets* for *shops*, *unhealthy* for *bad*). More formal language is needed (e.g. *a great deal* instead of *heaps*).

Spelling
Most words are spelt correctly. There are occasional errors that need correcting, (e.g. *individuals* is misspelt 'individuales'; *healthier* is misspelt 'healthiar').

The numeral *2* has been incorrectly used in place of the word *to*.

Note: words shaded in blue are errors.

UNIT TWO

Persuasive texts
Discussion essays

Understanding the question

Write an essay addressing the question below:

Zoos are cruel to wild animals. Discuss.

Type of question

This question is asking you to write a particular type of essay—a **discussion essay**.

The word *discuss* is your best clue that you need to write a discussion essay. To discuss means to consider **two sides** of a given topic and then conclude for **one side** or the other. This is different to an argument essay in which you are to select one side of an issue and support your side with evidence.

You are being asked to consider both points of view on zoos.

- Why do some people think zoos are cruel?
- Why do some people think zoos are not cruel?

Features of a discussion essay

- Aims to outline two sides of an issue and present a preferred side in the conclusion
- Has a broad structure with an introduction, body and conclusion
- Uses connectives to show the relationship between paragraphs and ideas
- Supports ideas with evidence
- Uses a range of common, collective and abstract nouns
- Uses formal and impersonal language

'Task words' tell you what you need to do in your piece of writing. These are usually verbs and act as instructions so that you know what is expected of you when writing a response to the topic.

explain examine compare contrast consider show discuss debate define evaluate

1 Underline the **task word** in the questions below. The first one has been done for you.

a People prefer salt to sugar. Discuss this statement with supporting evidence.

b Define the word *impede*.

c In 300 words, compare a family dinner to a football scrum.

d Outline how a car engine works.

e Evaluate the ending of *Harry Potter and the Deathly Hallows*.

f Explain how the circulatory system functions.

g Discuss whether or not teachers should be responsible for student happiness.

h Use a diagram to illustrate how the human heart works.

i Write a review of your favourite film.

Planning and organisation

All great writers **plan**. The planning stage of writing helps you **develop your ideas** and make sure that your writing is structured in a way that helps your readers understand your ideas. Planning is very important for formal essays as they have a strict structure.

Activity 1

On the spider-map below, add all you know about the **essay topic**. Be sure to focus on reasons why some people may believe zoos are cruel to wild animals and why some people may believe zoos are not cruel to wild animals.

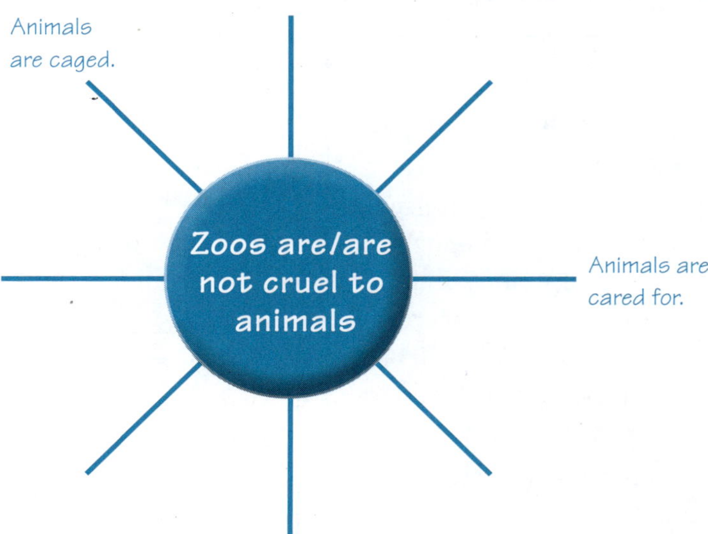

Activity 2

Use the library and the internet to conduct research on the topic. What are some **words or phrases** that might help you find information on the topic?

Some suggestions are: animal cruelty, animal welfare and animal rights.

Activity 3

Using the information from the spider-map above, complete the following table.

Question: Zoos are cruel to wild animals. Discuss.	
Yes	**No**

Structure

Discussion essays are formal pieces of writing. They have a very strict structure because the overall purpose of an essay is to **clearly outline a point of view** in relation to a particular question. It is important to learn the structure of an essay as you will be required to write many essays during your school years.

The basic **structure** of a discussion essay has three main parts: an **introductory** paragraph, **body** paragraphs and **concluding** paragraph. This helps you **organise your ideas** in response to the essay question. It is a good idea to have a really strong and clear structure as this helps your reader appreciate your understanding of the topic, as well as your ability to **construct a good argument**.

Introductory paragraph

The purpose of the introduction is to **provide an overview** of the essay topic and to **outline two different points of view** on this topic.

The basic introduction has three parts:

- a strong statement that **engages the reader** and **introduces the topic** of the essay; for example, a discussion essay about poetry may open with the statement,

  'Poetry expresses an individual's most intense emotions in just a few words.'
- one or two sentences that **provide more specific information** about the topic of the discussion essay
- a statement listing the **two sides of the topic** being discussed.

This is just one way of writing an introduction to a discussion essay. Learn this way and when you become more confident with writing essays you can write your introductions in a new way.

Activity 1

This student has written an **introduction to a discussion essay** responding to this statement:

We should spend less time texting. Discuss.

This introduction is jumbled up. **Sequence** the sentences so that they make a correctly structured introduction.

a Some people believe that we should spend less time text messaging but others feel that we do not need to limit the number of texts we send.

b Mobile phones have been part of our lives for the last 20 years.

c Since the late 1990s, Australians have been able to send text messages via their mobile phones and text messaging is now so popular that some young people send more than 100 texts per day.

Correct order: ______________________________

Activity 2

It is now time for you to draft your **introduction** to the discussion essay responding to the question *Zoos are cruel to wild animals. Discuss.*

Body paragraphs

The purpose of body paragraphs is to write detailed paragraphs outlining each argument **for** and **against** a given topic. Each paragraph will provide **evidence** to **support** each side of the argument being considered.

For this basic discussion essay you will only need to write two body paragraphs. However, these have a very clear **structure**:

1. a **statement** outlining the first point of view
2. an **example** to support this point of view
3. a **sentence** or two explaining how the example supports the first point of view
4. a **concluding sentence** that summarises this first point of view.

Your second paragraph will repeat the above structure but will focus on the second point of view. Once you become more confident writing essays you may choose to vary this structure.

Activity 3

In the example below, use the numbers 1 to 4 to identify the four parts of a **body paragraph**.

Some people believe that aliens exist and visit our planet. In 2012, thousands of people attended the 21st annual International UFO Congress. This conference had speakers from all over the world and people spent their time discussing their personal encounters with aliens as well as their theories about UFOs. From the large number of attendees at this conference, it is clear that many people do believe that aliens exist and visit our planet.

Activity 4

Look at this student's notes on the topic you've been given. Use your own paper to write one **body paragraph** using these notes. Remember that you should only discuss one side of the topic per paragraph so you will not need to use all of the notes. Look at the example discussion essay at the end of this unit if you get stuck!

* Zoos can treat animals badly.
* Animals may not be given appropriate care.
* Some people think zoos are cruel.
* Animals should be left in their habitat.
* Without appropriate care, animals can live painful lives which is very cruel.
* Animals may require protection from poachers and smugglers.
* Some people think zoos care for animals and are important.
* Zoos have very strict standards of animal care.

Concluding paragraph

The purpose of a **conclusion** is to provide a **summary** of each point of view and to present **unbiased support** for one of the points of view.

Your conclusion will have three parts:

1. a statement briefly listing **both sides** of the argument
2. a statement presenting **support for one of the sides** and briefly **justifying** this choice
3. a statement **summarising** which side of the argument you prefer and why.

Activity 5

Look at the conclusion below and use the numbers 1 to 3 to **identify the three parts** of a **discussion essay conclusion**.

The existence of aliens is disputed by many people, but some people believe that aliens exist and visit our planet. After considering both points of view it is obvious that there is limited credible evidence to support alien sightings and therefore it is highly unlikely that aliens have visited our planet. Therefore, in my view, aliens do not exist.

Activity 6

Draft the **concluding paragraph** for your discussion essay on the zoo topic, checking that you have included all three of the above elements.

Language feature

Connectives

Connectives are **linking words or phrases** that show the connections between ideas. In a discussion essay connectives such as *therefore* or *thus* are also used to express a conclusion. Look at this sentence to see how a connective can show a conclusion:

> In summary, people can be for or against coal-seam mining for a variety of reasons.

Connectives can be tricky to spell. Often a connective takes the form of an adverb (e.g. *lastly* or *similarly*). You can usually create an adverb by adding the suffix *ly* to the root word. See **Unit 1** for more details.

Connectives can also be used to show **contrast between ideas or positions** on a topic (e.g. *in contrast* or *alternatively*). Look at this sentence to see how a connective can show contrast:

> Coal-seam mining will provide the Australian natural resource industry with another valuable export. However, some people believe that coal-seam mining is extremely damaging to the environment.

Activity 1

Circle the connectives that express a **conclusion** and underline those that show **contrast**.

- **a** in summary
- **b** conversely
- **c** lastly
- **d** in contrast
- **e** to conclude
- **f** consequently
- **g** otherwise
- **h** thus
- **i** alternatively
- **j** nevertheless
- **k** on the other hand
- **l** however

Activity 2

Circle the correct connective from the two given in these sentences. You will need to decide whether the connective should show **conclusion** or **contrast** by reading the sentence closely.

- **a** Thirdly, playing video games is usually only one activity in a child's busy day. Consequently/Yet some people believe that playing video games is good for young people.
- **b** Eating chocolate is enjoyed by most Australians. In conclusion/Yet it is understandable why some people feel that eating chocolate is bad for your health.
- **c** It can be argued that whaling is a crime. However/In summary, some argue that it is a valued cultural practice.
- **d** Some people believe that dieting is bad for children. To conclude/Alternatively, some people believe that it is important for children to be weight conscious.

Activity 3

Below are two sentences that show different opinions about one topic. Select an appropriate connective to show the **contrast** between the two opinions and form one sentence. Select connectives from those given in Activity 1 on the previous page.

- **a** Chocolate is consumed in large quantities in Western countries. Confectionary such as lollies is very popular as well.
- **b** Skateboarding is an activity enjoyed by many young people. Adults believe that skateboarding is dangerous and risky.
- **c** Dogs are loyal animals that protect their owners fiercely. Cats are disloyal as they prefer ensuring their own comfort and security.

Spotlight *on spelling*

Plurals

When writing a discussion essay you will find that you need to use a variety of **plural nouns**. This is because in a discussion essay you will need to write about people and things in general. Spelling plural nouns is not always as easy as adding the suffix *s*. Three common suffixes you will need to add to transform a singular noun into a plural noun are *s*, *es* and *ies*.

Nouns ending in *o*, *ss*, *sh*, *ch* and *x* all require you to add the suffix *es* to create the plural form.

For example: hero → hero**es**, cross → cross**es**, wish → wish**es**, witch → witch**es**, fox → fox**es**

Nouns ending in *y* require you to drop the *y* and add the suffix *ies* to create the plural form.

For example: agency → agenc**ies**, charity → charit**ies**, rally → rall**ies**

Activity 1

Turn these singular nouns into **plural nouns** by adding *s*, *es* or *ies*.

- **a** zero ____________________
- **b** ghetto ____________________
- **c** memento ____________________
- **d** torpedo ____________________
- **e** embargo ____________________
- **f** jelly ____________________
- **g** eyelash ____________________
- **h** flash ____________________
- **i** theory ____________________

j study ______________________

k family ______________________

l leash ______________________

m gash ______________________

n absurdity ______________________

o accessory ______________________

p activity ______________________

q capability ______________________

r certainty ______________________

s library ______________________

t country ______________________

u faculty ______________________

v allergy ______________________

w approach ______________________

x attachment ______________________

y dispatch ______________________

z trench ______________________

Activity 2

Underline the words spelt incorrectly in each sentence and then write them correctly on the line.

a In their speechs given before the prime minister, Anh and Cai shared stories of their grandmother's important mementoes brought with her from Vietnam. ______________________

b Each year communities celebrate their local heros who make a difference. ______________________

c Some people believe that countrys with larger populations should pay high carbon emissions taxes. ______________________

d In conclusion, the evidence of the research companies supports the saving of endangered animales. ______________________

e On the contrary, some groups believe that the absurditys of the current government are an embarrassment. ______________________

f The theorys of Albert Einstein continue to be the focus of research for a number or physicists. ______________________

g The team of Australian experts was excited to be chasing tornados in the Central American deserts. ______________________

h Ultimately, the dwindling of food supplys for homeless and unemployed citizens was distressing the organisation. ______________________

You be the teacher

Below is a **body paragraph** for a discussion essay written by a Year 7 student. There are some errors in the structure of the paragraph and the spelling of some of the plurals. Improve the **structure** and rewrite the paragraph with the **correct spelling of all plurals**.

Consequently it is understandable why some people believe that zoos are not cruel because they may act as sanctuarys for endangered animals. Some people believe that zoos are not cruel. Zooes in citys do good work because they protect animales from poacheres who wish to harm the animals. Many animals in the wild are at risk of being hunted and killed by poachers.

Now you write

It is now time for you to complete your own **discussion essay** on the zoo topic.

1. Before you write, take some time to look at the student writing samples on the following pages as a guide to writing standards. Note the mistakes made in the Intermediate sample and try to avoid making these mistakes yourself.

2. Once you have read the two student writing samples, take some time to think about what you believe are the most important features of a discussion essay that you need to master. Use the lines below to jot down your answer to this question:

   What do you find most difficult when writing this kind of text?

3. Now look at the persuasive text marking criteria on page vii to double-check that you understand the requirements for a really good piece of persuasive writing.

   Remember that you have already done your planning and drafted your introductory paragraph, one body paragraph and concluding paragraph. Use your own paper. Good luck!

Looking at other students' writing

Write an essay addressing the question below:
The internet should replace libraries. Discuss.

ADVANCED SAMPLE

THE INTERNET SHOULD REPLACE LIBRARIES. DISCUSS.

The internet, which has been accessible to the public for over 20 years, is essentially a system of interconnected computers that allows for the sharing of information. Before the invention of the internet, people's main source of information was books, often accessed in libraries. Many believe that the internet will soon replace libraries. However, some people feel strongly that libraries will never be replaced entirely by the internet.

In Australia today, many people are beginning to argue that the internet should replace libraries. High schools in Australia have begun replacing their school libraries with rows of computers as well as mobile devices such as laptops and e-readers. As this trend shows, traditional libraries full of books are becoming unnecessary since the majority of information and books can now be accessed online. Thus it is understandable why many people feel that the internet should replace libraries.

Yet, it is believed by some that the internet should not replace libraries. Libraries continue to be popular places in the local community where individuals and groups access physical books for information and pleasure as well as access the internet at the library computers. This shows that libraries function as important community spaces as they allow people to access both the traditional and new sources of information and entertainment. Therefore it can be seen that many people feel that the internet should not replace libraries.

Some people feel that the internet should replace libraries as the majority of information can be accessed online while other people feel that the internet shouldn't replace libraries because they are important community spaces. After considering both points of view it is obvious libraries should not be replaced by the internet because they allow for access to both online and physical information. I have concluded, for the above reasons, that the internet should not replace libraries.

Introduction
The introduction immediately alerts the audience to the topic of the essay: the internet. It provides a detailed overview of the topic.
It clearly states both points of view—for and against the internet replacing libraries.

Persuasive techniques
The student uses language free of bias to outline each point of view. They use modals to show different degrees of certainty (e.g. *unnecessary* and *should*).

Text structure
The student uses the correct structure of a discussion essay, including an introduction, supporting paragraphs and a conclusion.

Paragraphing
Each paragraph features one point of view on the topic with evidence to support this reason.

Cohesion
The student uses connectives to show clear connections between ideas, especially to show ccontrast (e.g. *while*) and conclusion (e.g. *I have concluded*).

Vocabulary
The student's language choices are appropriate to their purpose—to discuss differing points of view on a topic. They use complex and precise words to talk about the topic.

Sentence structure
All sentences are grammatically correct, well structured and meaningful, and use a variety of sentence patterns.

Ideas
Ideas are well selected and relevant, with a lot of detail to support both points of view.

Punctuation
Correct punctuation is used throughout the argument.

Spelling
All words are spelt correctly, including plurals.

Write an essay addressing the question below:
The internet should replace libraries. Discuss.

Introduction
The student alerts the audience to the topic in first sentence. The student needs to provide more detailed information about the topic.

Vocabulary
The student's language is mostly appropriate to their purpose. More complex and exact vocabulary is needed (e.g. 'unnecessary' for 'don't need', 'interconnect' for 'hook up'). More formal language is needed (e.g. 'some people believe' instead of 'some people reckon').

INTERMEDIATE SAMPLE

THE INTERNET SHOULD REPLACE LIBRARIES. DISCUSS.

The internet is 20 years old and lets computers hook up to each other. Before the internet, people's used books at librarys for information. Some people think that there will be no libraries soon but some don't.

Some people reckon the internet should replace libraries. Some schools don't have libraries, they just have computer's with the internet. As this example shows, we don't need books anymore because computers are better. That's why people feel that the internet should replace libraries.

Some think that the internet should not replace libraries. Libraries give people a place to go to and they like to use computers and bookes there. As this example shows, libraries function as important community spaces as they allow people to access both the traditional and new sources of informmation and entertainment. Therefore it is understandable why many people feel that the internet should not replace libraries.

The internet should not replace libraries because they let people use both online and physical information. It is recommended for the above reasones that the internet does not replace libraries.

Ideas
The student's ideas are relevant to the argument. The ideas need more detail as they are quite general.

Persuasive techniques
Mostly uses language free of bias to outline each point of view.

Punctuation
Simple punctuation is mostly used correctly, but there are some errors in punctuation, including the incorrect use of possessive apostrophe (e.g. *people's* instead of *people*.

Text structure
The student uses the correct structure of a persuasive text including an introduction, supporting paragraphs and a conclusion. The student needs to further elaborate own position in the conclusion.

Cohesion
Connectives are used correctly.

Paragraphing
Each paragraph features one basic reason to support the point of view being discussed.

Paragraphs need to give more detail to support ideas especially paragraph two and the conclusion.

Sentence structure
The student uses a variety of simple and compound sentences but needs to include complex sentences that demonstrate a better control of language.

Spelling
Most words are spelt correctly. There are occasional errors that need correcting (e.g. *information* is misspelt 'informmation'; *reasons* is misspelt 'reasones' and *books* is misspelt 'bookes').

Note: words shaded in blue are errors.

UNIT THREE

Persuasive texts
Film reviews

Understanding the question

Film reviews:

Review an animated film that you have recently watched.

Type of question

This question is asking you to write a particular type of review—a **film review**.

A film review requires you to **evaluate** a film and **develop your own opinion** about whether it is worthy of being watched or not. In this question you are being asked to review an animated movie.

Features of a film review

- Aims to present an opinion about a film
- Attempts to convince the reader to see or not see the film in the concluding paragraph
- Supplies opinion with evidence and examples from the film
- Structure: introduction, body and conclusion
- Is typically divided into paragraphs on key aspects of a film (e.g. plot summary, character/actors, film style)
- Uses persuasive devices such as repetition, high modal language, evaluative adverbs, hyperbole, emotive language and humour

1 What does the word *review* mean?

____

____

____

2 What is a film?

____

____

____

3 What is an animated film?

____

____

____

4 Who is the target audience of most animated films? Why?

5 List all of the animated films you have seen recently.

Planning and organisation

The most important feature of a film review is your **judgement of the film**. When you judge a film, you determine what you like about it and what you don't like about it. From this you make a final judgement on the film as a whole—do you like it or don't you?

Planning a film review requires a close watching of the film and taking notes on plot, acting, ideas and film techniques as you watch.

Activity 1

Use the tables below to brainstorm your initial **response to the main elements** of the film you are planning to review. Think of this as being like writing a list of pros and cons.

Plot	
Good	**Bad**

Acting	
Good	**Bad**

Message of the film (e.g. growing up is hard; be nice to your family)	
Good	**Bad**

Film techniques	
Good	**Bad**

Activity 2

Read back over the information you added to the tables. From this information decide whether you feel more strongly that you **like** or you **dislike** the film. Write one sentence to explain why you have made this evaluation.

Activity 3

Write three points about each of these elements of a film to support your judgement in your **review** of the film (remember that your judgment means whether you think the film is good or bad).

For example: If you thought the film was bad you might say *terrible choice of actors, no chemistry between the lead actors* and *main actor was not funny even though he was meant to be.*

Acting	* * *
Film techniques	* * *
Plot	* * *
Ideas	* * *

Structure

Often **film reviews** look as if they don't have a strong structure but if you look closely you will see that they do follow a pattern. This **structure** helps organise the writer's opinion about the film and their evidence to support this opinion. Reviews have a similar structure to other persuasive texts: **introductory** paragraph, **body** paragraphs and **concluding** paragraph.

See **Unit 1** for more information on writing an engaging opening sentence for a persuasive text.

Introductory paragraph

The **opening paragraph** of a review provides general information about the film and sometimes gives the writer's **opinion** of the film. This general information includes the film's title, the release date, the name of the director and the main actors. The first sentence of an introduction should **hook the reader's attention** and encourage them to continue reading. Writers may use a strong statement of their opinion, a joke, a rhetorical question or an anecdote.

Activity 1

Complete this table for the animated film you have chosen to review.

General information	Your film
Film title	
Release date	
Director	
Main actors	

Activity 2

A student has written these sentences as an **introductory paragraph** for a film review. Unfortunately they are out of order. Correct them by numbering them 1 to 4.

a ________ The film is based on the first book of the series *The Hunger Games* by author Suzanne Collins.

b ________ *The Hunger Games* was directed by Gary Ross and was released into cinemas on March 22nd 2012.

c ________ It was well adapted by the director and the actors were very well selected to suit the characters.

d ________ The film has been hotly anticipated by fans of Suzanne Collins' highly acclaimed *The Hunger Games* trilogy.

Activity 3

It's now time for you to draft the **introductory paragraph** for your film review. Remember to go back through the planning you did earlier in the unit as this information will guide your writing.

Body paragraphs

The **body** of your film review is a series of paragraphs that **support** the reviewer's opinion with **evidence** from the film. Typically each paragraph focuses on a separate element of the film such as plot, quality of acting, film techniques or main ideas. Like all persuasive texts, you need to support your points with specific examples from the film.

Activity 4

Below are five sentences that a student has written for a **body paragraph** about acting. Draw a line through the two sentences that are not relevant to this paragraph.

1. The actors are very convincing in their roles.
2. The female lead actor is bad.
3. In the opening scene there is obvious chemistry between the two lead actors.
4. The male lead actor has a big nose.
5. The director has made a wonderful selection with the actors as all connect emotionally with the characters they are portraying.

Activity 5

Now that you have a good idea of what is required in a **body paragraph**. Have a go at writing your own body paragraphs for your film review. Remember to look at the example film review at the end of this unit to help you if you get stuck!

Concluding paragraph

This is the **final paragraph** of your film review and it is here that you really make your **evaluation** of it clear. In this paragraph you should once again mention the film being reviewed and encourage the reader to go and watch the film, or not go and watch the film.

Activity 6

It's now time for you to draft the **concluding paragraph** of your film review.

Language feature

Formal/informal language

The purpose of all film reviews is to present the writer's **evaluation** of the film and to **persuade** the reader to agree with the writer's evaluation. However, the language of a film review varies depending on the audience of the film review.

If the film review is to be published in an important film journal or magazine, then the **language** will be **formal** and the tone serious. If the film review is to be published in the local paper or on an entertainment website, then the language will be **informal** and the tone playful and conversational.

A film review typically features high modal language (see discussion of this in Unit 1), evaluative adverbs and hyperbole.

Film reviews are evaluative texts—they look closely at a film, evaluate its strength and weaknesses and then use this to develop an opinion on how good or bad a film is. Some adverbs can be used to express the attitude of a writer—we call these **evaluative adverbs**.

For example: The director **cleverly** uses a song with a strong guitar riff to create action in the opening scene.

In this example the adverb *cleverly* expresses the attitude of the writer towards the use of a song in the film.

Some commonly used **adverbs** include *cleverly, clearly, thankfully, predictably, importantly, happily, shamefully, strangely, surprisingly, appropriately, amazingly, understandably, sadly, unfortunately, funnily* and *regrettably*.

Activity 1

Circle the **adverbs** in the sentences below.

- **a** The director absurdly encourages the actors to look beyond the camera in every shot.
- **b** Angelina Jolie plays the annoyingly confident Mrs Black.
- **c** There are times when Kristen Stewart is just wandering around aimlessly in the woods.
- **d** Curiously, the ballroom is flooded by green lighting yet this enhances the eerie mood of the scene.
- **e** The second half of this film is disappointingly slow.

Activity 2

Select an **evaluative adverb** to fill the gap in one of these sentences. Remember that an adverb usually comes before a verb.

brilliantly	luckily
inexplicably	oddly

- **a** The director ______________________ has dedicated five minutes to a montage of ants at the beginning of the film.
- **b** This is Paris Hilton's feature film debut and ______________________ for viewers she is killed off early in the first half of the film.
- **c** The exquisite comedic timing of Stephen Fry ______________________ saves the film from being just another rom-com.
- **d** Witches and wizards are living in London and ______________________ enough we viewers can't help but falling in love with three of them—Harry, Ron and Hermione.

Often reviewers use **exaggeration** to persuade the reader to accept their position on the film. Exaggeration is often created using a rhetorical device called **hyperbole**. Hyperbole is a form of metaphor that intentionally exaggerates an experience and is not meant to be taken seriously.

For example: The bag weighed a tonne.

In this example the writer encourages the reader to imagine the bag being very heavy by suggesting that it weighs a tonne even though it is more likely that it is just heavier than usual.

Activity 3

Underline the use of **hyperbole** in the sentences below.

- **a** The film is worse than having a hoard of wild monkeys let loose in your living room.
- **b** It's hard to keep watching after Bella heaves her ten-thousandth sigh over her love, Edward.
- **c** This movie is so fast paced that I don't think a jet plane would be able to keep up.
- **d** Spielberg has poured so much money into the budget of this film you can occasionally see a hundred-dollar bill fall from the screen.

Activity 4

In each of the following examples of **hyperbole**, two things are being compared. Identify which two things are being compared and try to explain why this comparison has been used.

- **a** Keira Knightley looks as thin as a toothpick in this film, making her a very poor role model for young viewers. ______________________

____

- **b** The film stars the wonderful George Clooney who looks great even though he is as old as the hills.

____

____

- **c** Harry Potter actor Daniel Radcliffe is like a knight in shining armour in his new film.

____

____

Activity 5

Look back at the planning you did for your film review earlier in this unit. Use this information to write a **hyperbole** to describe each of the following.

a acting ______________________________

____

b film techniques ______________________________

____

c plot ______________________________

____

Spotlight *on spelling*

Prefixes

A **prefix** stands before a word and alters the meaning of the root word. A prefix cannot stand alone and is always spelt in full.

For example: *un* + cover → **un**cover

Common prefixes are *un, in, im, ir, de* and *sub*.

Prefixes

Some examples of words using prefixes include *disjoint, discover, devalue, defame, submerge, inappropriate, incapable, inside, irreplaceable, irresponsible, irregular* and *impossible.*

Adjectives and prefixes

Adjectives are important when writing film reviews as they communicate the writer's **attitude** about the film. Many adjectives are root words with **prefixes** and suffixes added. See Unit 4 for more information on suffixes.

Activity 1

Add a **prefix** (*un, ir, de* or *im*) to turn these words into their opposites. The first one has been done for you.

a responsible ___irresponsible___

b rational ____________

c possible ____________

d regular ____________

e relevant ____________

f reverent ____________

g resistible ____________

h afraid ____________

i affordable ____________

j broken ____________

k excited ____________

l grateful ____________

m imaginative ____________

n intelligent ____________

o active ____________

p brief ____________

Activity 2

Circle the correct **adjective/adverb** from the two options given to complete each sentence.

- **a** Some people will argue that opening your front door to a group of zombies is (unintelligent/unnintelligent); I would agree.
- **b** Dedicated film enthusiasts and vampire buffs will undoubtedly spend hours trying to (deconstruct/decconstruct) Tim Burton's latest film.
- **c** It is (imppossible/impossible) not to love the first film in *The Hunger Games* trilogy.
- **d** Johnny Depp plays an (irational/irrational) barber who enjoys killing his clients.

Verbs and prefixes

Verbs are also important when writing film reviews as they are used to **show cause and effect**, especially in relation to the use of film techniques. Many verbs are root words with **prefixes** added.

Activity 3

Add a **prefix** (*dis*, *sub*, *im* or *em*) to change the form of these words to make them into **verbs**. The first one has been done for you.

- **a** tract ___distract___
- **b** let ______
- **c** divide ______
- **d** scribe ______
- **e** body ______
- **f** able ______
- **g** believe ______
- **h** connect ______
- **i** appear ______
- **j** balm ______
- **k** close ______
- **l** plant ______
- **m** brace ______
- **n** pale ______
- **o** figure ______
- **p** bed ______
- **q** approve ______
- **r** appoint ______

Activity 4

Circle the correct **verb** from the two options given to complete each sentence.

- **a** Some parents may (disapprove/dissaprove) of their children watching violence on screen, even if it is only between two cartoon characters.
- **b** Some children (dissbelieve/disbelieve) the myths of fairies found in picture books, but the film *Fairytale* can turn the most avid sceptic into a believer.
- **c** This film is so engaging for young viewers that parents will find it hard to get their children to (dissconnect/disconnect) from the screen.
- **d** With films as action-packed and funny as *Kung Fu Panda*, it isn't necessary to (subscribe/subbscribe) to a pay TV service.

You be the teacher

Below is a **body paragraph** for a film review written by a Year 7 student. There are some errors in the structure of the paragraph and the spelling of some of the **adverbs** and the words with **prefixes**. Improve the **structure** and rewrite the paragraph with the **correct spelling of all words**.

The action sequences in *The Incredibles* are nothing short of inccredible. While it lacks the gimmick factor of the big 3D films, it certainlly doesn't lack action and plot. The director cleverlly contrasts the unninteresting domestic life of the Parr family with the thrills and danger of the superhero life. It's immpossible not to be carried along with Mr Incredible as he attempts to live a double life and relive his glory days as a superhero.

Now you write

It is now time for you to complete your own **film review** on an animated film.

1. Before you write, take some time to look at the student writing samples on the following pages as a guide to writing standards. Note the mistakes made in the Intermediate sample and try to avoid making these mistakes yourself.

2. Once you have read the two student writing samples, take some time to think about what you believe are the most important features of a film review that you need to master. Use the lines below to jot down your answer to this question:

   What do you find most difficult when writing this kind of text?

3. Now look at the persuasive text marking criteria on page vii to double-check that you understand the requirements for a really good piece of persuasive writing.

   Remember that you have already done your planning and drafted your introductory paragraph, one body paragraph and concluding paragraph. Use your own paper. Good luck!

Looking at other students' writing

Film reviews:

Write a review of a comedy film.

Introduction
The introduction immediately alerts the audience to the film being reviewed. The student uses humour in the first sentence to engage the reader.
The introduction clearly outlines general information about the film.

Persuasive techniques
The language of opinion is used and supported with examples. The student uses adverbs to evaluate the film (e.g. *unlikely* and *mostly*).

Text structure
The correct structure of a film review is used, including an introduction, supporting paragraphs and a conclusion.

Paragraphing
Each paragraph focuses on a separate element of the film. The main points are supported with examples from the film.

Cohesion
The student uses pronouns to replace nouns once they are introduced to avoid repetition (e.g. *this* and *it*).

ADVANCED SAMPLE

MY BIG FAT GREEK WEDDING—PG, DIRECTED BY JOEL ZWICK

The title of this movie speaks for itself. There isn't much more to this Hollywood romantic comedy other than a big, fat Greek wedding. The director, Joel Zwick, has done the best he can to make something out of nothing, but ultimately this film spends an hour and a half going nowhere. *My Big Fat Greek Wedding* gives the viewer some laughs, but ultimately fails due to the poor choice of actors.

The plot revolves around Toula—a daggy, 30-year-old Greek woman who is unhappy with life. Toula works at her parents' Greek restaurant and is watching her life slip by when she serves schoolteacher, Ian Miller. It's easy to see that this is love at first sight but the director introduces a variety of unlikely problems to make the relationship between the two difficult. The biggest obstacle is Toula's Greek heritage because her parents want her to marry a Greek man. This conflict is the main action of the film.

There are a few funny moments in this film where the acting is very good. One particular scene that gets a laugh is the slap-stick routine of Toula when she tangles herself in the telephone headpiece at her new job in the travel agency. Unfortunately the film is mostly cast with average actors who play their roles without passion.

While the film doesn't have a strong plot or quality actors, it does have an important message for the viewers. The need to accept individuals for who they are is strongly presented in this film. Toula's family is shown to be different from most American families yet despite this they are happy.

My Big Fat Greek Wedding is the type of film you watch on television when there is nothing else better to watch. Tired mums and bored dads will get a few laughs from this feel-good film. Watch this film when you're desperate.

Vocabulary
The choice of language is appropriate to the student's purpose—to evaluate the film. The use of technical terms is appropriate to the film (e.g. plot, comedic moments).

Sentence structure
All sentences are grammatically correct, well structured and meaningful. The student uses a variety of sentence patterns.

Ideas
Ideas are well selected and relevant, with a lot of detail to support the student's opinion of the film.

Punctuation
Correct punctuation is used throughout the review.

Spelling
All words are spelt correctly, including plurals.

Film reviews:

Write a review of a comedy film.

Introduction
The introduction alerts the audience to the student's opinion of the film in the first sentence. The introduction needs to provide more detailed information about the film.

Sentence structure
The student uses a variety of simple and compound sentences. They need to include complex sentences that demonstrate a better control of language.

INTERMEDIATE SAMPLE

MY BIG FAT GREEK WEDDING

This movie is just about a big, fat Greek wedding. The movie was released way back in 2002 and you can tell! Joel Zwick is the director and he tries hard to make the film funny but it doesn't work. *My Big Fat Greek Wedding* is sometimes funny but mostly it is boring.

The story is about a Greek woman, Toula, who is unhappy and then she meets a guy, Ian, who makes her happy. It is made clear that the two will fall in love even though the director includes a lot of unlikely problems for them. Because Toula is Greek and Ian isn't, her parents don't want them to get married and this causes problems.

Some parts have really good acting and this makes the audiense laugh. There are funny scenes where people hurt themselves.

The film does have a good message for the audience. The film tells us that it isn't impossible to get along with other cultures and we should try to discover new ways of seeing the world. Toulas' family are happy with their Greek heritadge but they are still excepting of Ian who is not Greek.

I would only watch *My Big Fat Greek Wedding* if everything else on television was really boring. *My Big Fat Greek Wedding* would be good for bored people because it isn't very funny but is kind of funny.

Vocabulary
The language used is mostly appropriate to the student's purpose. More complex and exact vocabulary is needed. Less causal language is required (e.g. *she meets a nice man* instead of *she meets a guy*.

Persuasive techniques
The student mostly uses the language of opinion to evaluate the film. More adverbs are needed to show a detailed evaluation of the film.

Paragraphing
Each paragraph features one element of the film.
Paragraphs need to give more detailed examples to support the student's opinion of the film.

Ideas
The student uses good ideas that are relevant to the argument. Their ideas need more detail as they are quite general. The third paragraph is far too brief.

Cohesion
There is occasional use of pronouns to replace nouns, but too much unnecessary repetition of the main nouns (e.g. *the film* and the title *My Big Fat Greek Wedding*.

Text structure
The student follows the correct structure of a film review, including an introduction, supporting paragraphs and a conclusion.

Spelling
Most words are spelt correctly. Occasional errors need correcting, including words such as 'audiense' instead of *audience*, 'heritadge' instead of *heritage* and 'excepting' instead of *accepting*.

Punctuation
Simple punctuation is mostly used correctly. There are some errors in punctuation, including the incorrect use of possessive apostrophe (e.g. *Toulas'* instead of *Toula's*.)

Note: words shaded in blue are errors.

UNIT FOUR

Persuasive texts
Blog posts

Understanding the question

Write a blog post using the title below:
Reality television is overrated.

Type of question

This question is asking you to write a particular type of persuasive text—a **blog post**. The word *blog* is short for web log. A blog post is essentially a short piece of writing that focuses on a topic of personal interest and is published on the internet via a blog site. Blogs allow for readers to respond to the writer's ideas via comments below the post.

How do you know what to write about? The title of a blog post tells the readers what the post will be about. Here, you are being asked to write a post about why reality television is overrated.

Features of a blog post

- Expresses an opinion about a particular issue
- Often aims to influence the way the audience thinks and behaves
- Argues for or against a particular issue
- Supports ideas with evidence
- Has a loose structure: introduction, body and conclusion
- Uses persuasive, emotive and descriptive language, and uses both first-person and second-person narrative
- Should be highly engaging with a strong personal voice
- Uses rhetorical questions to include the reader

1 The question given includes two key **content words** that tell you what you must focus on in your speech. Write a brief definition of each. You might want to use a dictionary to help you.

Look back at Unit 1 on page 1 to find out about **content words**.

a reality television ______________________________

____

____

b overrated ______________________________

____

____

2 Find two **synonyms** (words that mean the same or similar in meaning) for the adjective *overrated*.

____

Planning and organisation

Often in the **planning** stage you may write more notes than are needed in the finished written piece. After brainstorming you must select the points you think are your best!

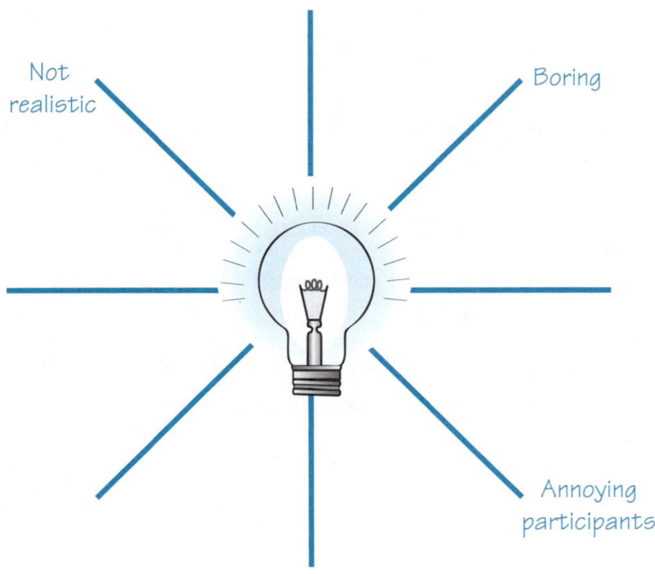

Activity 1

Using the spider-map above, **brainstorm** all you know about the blog post topic.

Activity 2

Use the information you have gathered so far to write three clear sentences that state why you think **reality television is overrated**.

a ______________________________

b ______________________________

c ______________________________

Structure

You've done your planning; now it's time to look at the structure and key language features of a **blog post**.

As with all persuasive texts, the **structure** of a blog post is typically composed of an **introduction**, **body** paragraphs and **conclusion**. However, a blog post is an **informal**, personal form of writing and sometimes one or more of these elements may not be fully developed.

Introduction

The **introduction** to a blog post does not have a strict structure, but it does have one important rule: it must be **engaging** so that your reader keeps reading and doesn't skip to another web page. You can create an engaging introduction using similar methods to those of a persuasive speech: a strong statement, a statistic, a joke, an anecdote or a rhetorical question. Of course this first sentence should relate to the title and topic of your blog post. It's a good idea to **outline your main points** in your introduction as well.

Activity 1

Below are a series of **blog post introductions** on a variety of different topics. Match each type of engaging introduction with its correct example. The first one has been done for you.

a statement	Who wouldn't love to spend every waking hour reading a book?
b statistic	Yesterday, for five hours solid, I was held captive on my lounge—I couldn't put my book down!
c joke	Young people between 8 to 18 years of age spend nearly 4 hours a day in front of a television screen.
d anecdote	What type of building has the most stories? A library!
e rhetorical question	I firmly believe that reading a book is far superior to watching television.

Activity 2

In the following example of a good **introduction**, circle the engaging opening and underline the main points that the blog post will cover.

It's impossible to get quality pizza in Australia! Once I had believed that our pizza was satisfying but last year I travelled to New York City and my appreciation for this take-away favourite was altered forever. Coming home to Oz, I've discovered that there are a few things that Australian pizza must work on: size, crust and toppings.

Activity 3

Draft the **introduction** to your blog post titled *Reality television is overrated.* Remember to use your notes from the planning stage!

Body paragraphs

The **body** of a blog post is made up of a series of paragraphs. Each paragraph deals with a separate point connected to the topic being discussed and **provides evidence** to **support** this point. This evidence may take the form of anecdotes (personal stories used to illustrate a point), personal observations or quotes from a variety of sources.

Activity 4

Match each type of **evidence** with its correct example.

a quote	People seem to be passionate about writing; if they weren't we wouldn't have all of the wonderful books in our libraries.
b personal observation	Just yesterday my little brother attempted to write his first story—it was only four jumbled words—but he was so excited with his work!
c anecdote	One of my favourite quotes about writing is by George Orwell who said, 'Writing a book is a horrible, exhausting struggle, like a long bout of some painful illness.'

Activity 5

Go back to the notes you made during the planning stage and draft one **body paragraph** for your blog post.

Conclusion

The **conclusion** of a blog post is very important as it **sums up your argument**. This is also where you encourage your reader to respond to your points by adding their own views as a comment below your post—this is often referred to as a 'conversation'. Lots of bloggers (people who write blogs regularly) end their posts by asking a question directly to their readers.

For example: What things do you do each day that help protect the environment from further damage?

Activity 6

Draft the **conclusion** for your blog post. Don't forget to finish with a question directed at your audience!

Language feature

Rhetorical questions

Blog posts are a personal and **informal** form of writing. They aim to engage readers by directly addressing them throughout. This encourages readers to think in a new way about a topic. A great technique to encourage readers to think is to ask a rhetorical question.

A **rhetorical question** is a form of question that doesn't require a direct response from the reader—it is a **thinking** question and is often used to **reassert the writer's position**.

An example of a rhetorical question is *How will we ever stop people polluting?* The purpose of this question is to get people thinking about the problem of pollution and possible solutions for this problem.

Activity 1

Match each **rhetorical question** to its blog post topic. The first one has been done for you.

a pizza	How can we continue to live our lives as though there is no suffering in this world?
b mobile phones	When was the last time you took a really good look in your wardrobe?
c school	Could you live for three days without texting?
d poverty	Why can't Australians make a good pizza?
e fashion	Is it possible to enjoy a single day of school?

Activity 2

Write a **rhetorical question** about the given topic using the question openings provided. The first one has been done for you.

a Sentence starter: Why is it that …

Topic: Chocolate

Rhetorical question: Why is it that there are so many different types of chocolate?

b Sentence starter: When will people …

Topic: Recycling

Rhetorical question: ______________________________

c Sentence starter: Wouldn't it be great if …

Topic: Dogs

Rhetorical question: ______________________________

d Sentence starter: Don't you think …

Topic: Video games

Rhetorical question: ______________________________

Activity 3

Choose the correct sentence opening to help change the sentences below into **rhetorical questions** for your blog post. You may need to slightly change the wording of the original sentence. Don't forget that a question ends with a question mark!

Did you know that …	Isn't it about time that …	Is it possible that …	Should …

a Reality television is bad for Australian actors. ______________________________

b Mobile phone companies profit from reality television programs. ______________________________

c Australian viewers should demand better quality television. ______________________________

d Reality television gives everyday people the chance to be a 'star'. ______________________________

Irregular plurals

When writing a blog post you will find you need to use a variety of plural nouns. In the last unit you learnt about plurals. But did you know that there are some nouns which have irregular plural endings? We call these words **irregular plurals**. You might notice that most of these irregular plurals are words that have come from foreign languages like Latin, Greek or French!

Here are some examples:

Nouns that end in *us* change the suffix to *i* to create the plural.

radi**us** → radi**i**
nucle**us** → nucle**i**

Nouns ending in *is* change the suffix to *es* to create the plural.

hypothes**is** → hypothes**es**
synthes**is** → synthes**es**

Nouns ending in *ix* change the suffix to *ices* to create the plural.

append**ix** → append**ices**
matr**ix** → matr**ices**

Nouns ending in *eau* change the suffix to *eaux* to create the plural.

bur**eau** → bur**eaux**
tabl**eau** → tabl**eaux**

Nouns ending in *a* change the suffix to *ae* to create the plural.

antenn**a** → antenn**ae**
vertebr**a** → vertebr**ae**

Nouns ending in *um* change the suffix to *a* to create the plural.

bacteri**um** → bacteri**a**
dat**um** → dat**a**

Some nouns make no changes at all; their singular and plural forms are the same.

species → species
series → series
means → means

Activity 1

Underline the incorrectly spelt **irregular plurals** and then rewrite them correctly.

a Our English teacher asked us to write three different thesises for homework. ________________

b Having great difficulty with his formulaes, Lee decided to take a break. ________________

c The Gold Coast is viewed as one of a number of northern oasises for people who live down south. ________________

d Multiple stimuluses in the classroom can distract students. ________________

e The director of the education department was frustrated by the number of different curriculuums the schools needed to use. ________________

Activity 2

Make these singular nouns into **plural nouns**.

a medium ____________________

b stimulus ____________________

c diagnosis ____________________

d axis ____________________

e analysis ____________________

f focus ____________________

g sheep ____________________

h thesis ____________________

i datum ____________________

j synopsis ____________________

Activity 3

Complete this table of **singular** and **plural nouns**.

Singular noun	Plural noun
index	
	beaux
crisis	
	cacti
medium	

You be the teacher

Below is a **body paragraph** for a blog post written by a Year 7 student. There are some errors in the structure of the paragraph and the spelling of some of the **irregular plurals**. Improve the **structure** and rewrite the paragraph with the **correct spelling of all words**.

I just hope that Australians overcome this reality obsession soon. Our fixation with reality television is one of Australia's biggest cultural crisises. Australia has some extremely talented creative artists—screenwriters, actors, designers—who could fill our screenes with wonderfully fictitious television serieses and films. Don't you think it odd that we would sit for hours and hours watching other everyday people cook, clean, sing, dance or paint a house? I spend enough time in reality with all of its boring and messy bits.

Now you write

It is now time for you to complete your own **blog post** on reality television.

1 Before you write, take some time to look at the student writing samples on the following pages as a guide to writing standards. Note the mistakes made in the Intermediate sample and try to avoid making these mistakes yourself.

2 Once you have read the two student writing samples, take some time to think about what you believe are the most important features of a blog post that you need to master. Use the lines below to jot down your answer to this question:

What do you find most difficult when writing this kind of text?

3 Now look at the persuasive text marking criteria on page vii to double-check that you understand the requirements for a really good piece of persuasive writing.

Remember that you have already done your planning and drafted your introduction, one body paragraph and conclusion. Use your own paper. Good luck!

Looking at other students' writing

Write a blog addressing the statement below:

Books are better than television.

ADVANCED SAMPLE

BLOG: BOOKS ARE BETTER THAN TELEVISION.

What do monsters, aliens, detectives and dinosaurs all have in common? They can all be found inside the pages of a book. I've always believed that books are one of the best ways to beat boredom and much more rewarding than television. Why wouldn't I think that? Reading gives us control over what we imagine. There is no limit to the variety of books available, from fantasy to history. I always sleep well if I read before I go to bed, but if I watch television before bed my sleep is disrupted.

Books give us the power to imagine new characters, events and places. When I was little I used to love *The Hobbit* because I would be transported into a world of dwarves, dragons and hairy-footed hobbits. We readers must use our imaginations to create pictures of these creatures. Books give people the freedom of imagination—something we can all be happy about.

It's not just the freedom of imagination that I love about books—they also provide us with endless experiences. A visit to your local library or bookshop will present you with a variety of choices. Do you want to read fiction or non-fiction? Horror, romance, young adult, comedy, science fiction? As Dr Seuss once said, 'The more you read, the more things you will know. The more that you learn, the more places you'll go.' There really is a book to suit everyone's taste and that's something television can't offer.

Have you ever really considered the impact that books and television have on your mind? My parents stopped me from watching television in bed, and for good reason. Watching television late into the night can significantly impact sleeping patterns. A good book in bed on the other hand can lead to a peaceful sleep by relaxing your body and mind before you drift off. I have always thanked my parents for my peaceful sleep.

You may never have thought this closely about books and television before, but after reading this, I do hope you elect to choose a book over the television. Books are vastly better than television because they free the imagination and help relax a restless mind. So, will you go and turn off the screen and pick up a book?

Introduction
The student engages the reader in the topic immediately by using a rhetorical question.

Persuasive techniques
The student uses inclusive language (e.g. vwe and readers) to connect with the reader. Second-person narrative has been used to encourage thought (e.g. *Have you ever really considered …*) Descriptive language engages the reader in the ideas of the post (e.g. *transported into a world of dwarves, dragons and hairy-footed hobbits*).

Text structure
The student uses the correct structure of a speech, including an introduction, supporting paragraphs and a conclusion.

Paragraphing
Each paragraph features one basic reason to support the point of view and evidence to support this reason. Evidence is a quote, an anecdote or a personal observation.

Cohesion
Each paragraph opens with a strong sentence that indicates the idea to be discussed.

Vocabulary
Language choices are appropriate to the student's purpose—to engage the reader in a discussion of the value of books over television. Complex and precise words are used to talk about the topic.

Sentence structure
All sentences are grammatically correct, well structured and meaningful. There is a variety of sentence patterns.

Ideas
Ideas are well selected and relevant, with a lot of detail to support the speaker's position—books are better than television.

Punctuation
Correct punctuation is used throughout the argument.

Spelling
All words are spelt correctly.

Write a blog addressing the statement below:

Books are better than television.

Introduction
The student alerts the audience to their point of view in the first sentence and summarises their position. They need to grab the audience's attention more effectively with a rhetorical question.

Sentence structure
The student uses a variety of simple and compound sentences. They need to include complex sentences that demonstrate a better control of language.

INTERMEDIATE SAMPLE

BLOG: BOOKS ARE BETTER THAN TELEVISION.

Books are better than television and are one of the best ways to not get bored. I think they let you experience something new with the turn of a page. Reading lets us use our imaginations. There are so many books to read about all sorts of topics. You can even take a book to bed with you which better than watching television. Books are better.

Books help us imagine new things. I read *The Hobbit* and it has dwarves, dragons, hobbits and. We must use our imaginashun to see these creatures not like with television where it is shown to us. Books let us imagine.

Books also provide us with different types of experiences. Writers always say that books give us new experiences. We can read horror, romance, young adult, comedy, science fiction and more. There are heaps of book types we could be reading forever and this is exciting. Books give lots of choice but television only has a few programs so we don't get much choice.

Books are better for your brain than television. Most kids aren't allowed to have televisions in their rooms, my parents stopped me. This is because it can stop you from sleeping. but books are better because they help you fall asleep and relax. This makes books better than television.

I would like you to read books more than you watch television. Books help your imagination, have lots of varietys to suit everyone and help you relax. Books are better than television and all other mediums.

Ideas
The student's ideas are relevant to the argument. The ideas need more detail as they are quite general (e.g. *Books are better*).

Persuasive techniques
The student uses some inclusive language to connect with the reader. The sample does not use descriptive language to engage the reader. Verbs need to be less simplistic (e.g. *exciting* could be *exhilarating*.)

Vocabulary
The language used is mostly appropriate to the student's purpose. More complex and exact vocabulary is needed (e.g. *discouraged* for *stopped*, *multitude* for *heaps*.)

Paragraphing
Each paragraph features one basic reason to support the student's point of view.

The paragraphs need to give more detail to support ideas, especially paragraph three.

Cohesion
Each paragraph opens with a basic sentence that indicates the idea to be discussed. There needs to be more variety in the sentence beginnings.

Text structure
The student uses the correct structure of a persuasive text including an introduction, supporting paragraphs and a conclusion. They need to conclude with a thinking question.

Spelling
Most words are spelt correctly. Occasional errors need correcting (e.g. *varieties* is misspelt 'varietys'; *imagination* is misspelt 'imaginashun').

Irregular plurals are misspelt (e.g. *media* is misspelt 'mediums').

Punctuation
Simple punctuation is mostly used correctly but there are some errors in punctuation (e.g. missing capital letter, incorrect use of possessive apostrophe and sentences run together, such as *Most kids aren't allowed to have televisions in their rooms, my parents stopped me.*).

Note: words shaded in blue are errors.

UNIT FIVE

Informative texts
Procedures

Understanding the question

Write a procedure addressing the question below:
What is the best way to treat a bee sting?

Type of question

This question is asking you to write a particular type of informative text—a **procedure**. A procedure is a piece of writing that provides the reader with a series of steps to follow in order to complete a specific task.

You are being asked to write a series of steps showing how to treat a bee sting.

Features of a procedure

- Aims to tell the reader what to do and how to do it
- States the goal of the procedure in the title or first sentence
- Gives a series of steps to follow
- Often has numbered steps (1, 2, 3, etc.)
- Lists the materials needed
- Focus of procedure is factual
- Technical, scientific and complex words used
- Imperative verbs used
- Very few adjectives
- Short, precise sentences

1 Use a dictionary to define the word *procedure*.

____

____

2 List five other activities for which you may be asked to write a **procedure**.
For example: baking a cake.

a ____________________________________

b ____________________________________

c ____________________________________

d ____________________________________

e ____________________________________

Planning and organisation

Planning for a procedure helps you better organise the steps needed to complete the activity!

Activity 1

Use the two spider-maps below to **brainstorm** what you already know about the equipment and steps needed for treating a bee sting.

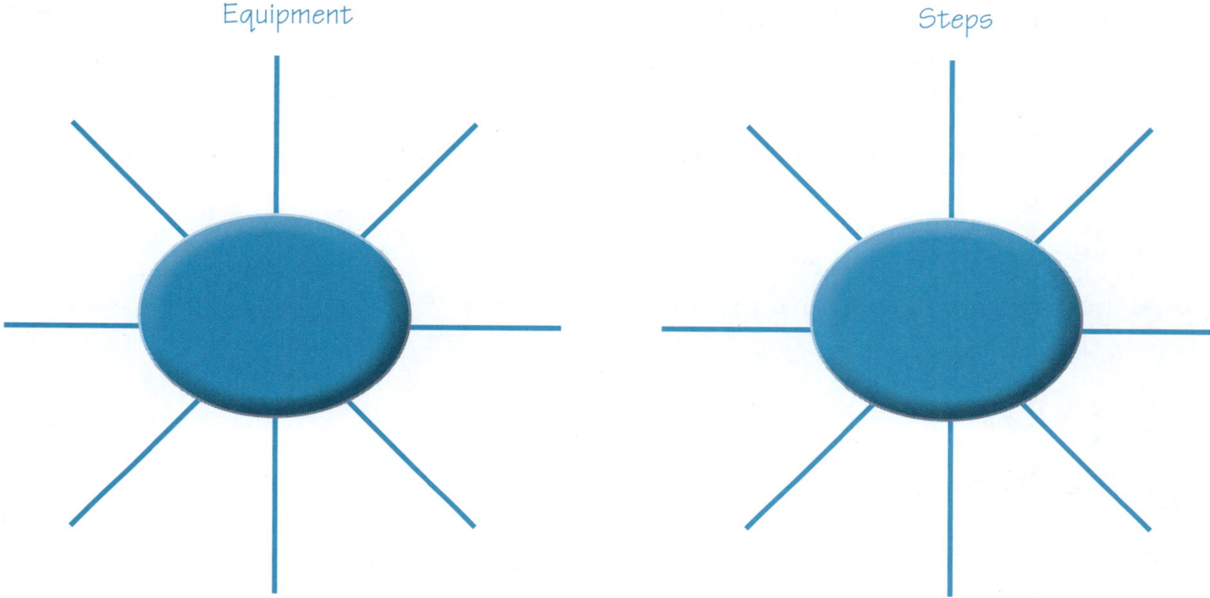

Activity 2

Now it's time to do some research. Research is helpful even if you are experienced in treating bee stings!

a Ask a friend or family member what they know about the **steps** and equipment involved in this activity. Record your notes from the conversation in the box below.

b Use the internet to discover more information about the **steps** and equipment involved in this activity. Remember to search for key words and don't rely on just the first few results from your search. Always make sure your source is reliable by checking the credibility of the writer and the date of publication. Record your notes from your research in the box below.

Structure

You've done your planning; now it's time to look at the structure and a key language feature of a procedure—**imperative sentences**.

You may not be aware of it, but we encounter **procedures** every day. When you read the **instructions** on the back of a cake mix or you watch a walk-through on YouTube of your favourite video game, you're engaging with a procedure. Procedures are important because they help us **successfully complete a range of activities**—from the very simple to the very complex. The procedure that you have to write for this unit is a simple one—how to treat a bee sting. However, the same **structure** and language features are used for more complex procedures such as replacing the ink cartridge in a printer.

All procedures begin with a **clear title** or **statement of the procedure's goal**. This is then followed by a very short paragraph that includes:

- a **reason** why this procedure is needed
- **information** that your reader may need to know before completing the procedure
- any safety **issues** to consider.

For example:

Washing a dog

It is important to know how to wash a dog because as a dog owner this is a task you will be doing frequently. Before washing your dog you should change into old clothes because dog washing can get messy! Always be sure that your dog is calm and confident before you wash it because scared dogs can quickly become aggressive.

Activity 1

Complete the following table to help you structure your **overview paragraph**.

Why do people need to learn how to treat bee stings?	
What important things might people need to know about treating bee stings before they begin?	
What safety issues should people consider before treating a bee sting?	

The **Equipment** section is where you list any **supplies** or **resources** that are needed to carry out the procedure. This will take the form of a list of items that indicates the number of each item required.

For example:

- 1 dog bath or large tub
- 1 bottle of dog shampoo
- 1 towel
- dog treats.

Activity 2

Go back to your research and planning from earlier and write the list of **equipment** you will need to treat a bee sting. Remember to be **precise** and **specific** about what is needed!

The rest of the procedure is simply a list of **steps** that the reader must follow in order to complete the activity. These steps are given **sequentially**—this means the steps are listed in the order they need to be taken. Remember that each step should take the form of a short, precise sentence—don't leave any step out! A procedure may include **numbered steps**, or the steps may use **connectives** like *first*, *next*, *then* and *finally*.

See **Unit 2** for more information on **connectives**.

Activity 3

A student has written this **procedure** about making a cake. Unfortunately the steps are not in the right order. Number the sentences correctly from 1 to 6. You may want to remove one or two unnecessary steps.

a ____________ Pour the combined mixture into a cake tin.

b ____________ Break the eggs into the bowl.

c ____________ Pour the milk onto the dry ingredients.

d ____________ Bake the cake for approximately 20 minutes.

e ____________ Preheat the oven to 180 degrees.

f ____________ Pour the dry cake mixture into a mixing bowl.

Activity 4

Now it's time to begin **structuring** your own procedure about how to treat a bee sting. Use the scaffold below (and your notes from the previous planning activity) to help you.

Title/goal:	
Overview:	
Equipment:	
Step one:	Step two:
Step three:	Step four:
Step five:	Step six:

Language feature

Imperative sentences

Procedures use a specific type of sentence that instructs the reader called an **imperative sentence**. Imperative sentences give a **command**—they ask or tell people to do something.

For example: **Place** two cups of shampoo into a bucket of lukewarm water.

Imperative sentences often begin with an imperative verb. This tells the reader the action that must be done. The imperative verb in the previous example has been highlighted.

Activity 1

Underline the **imperative verbs** in these sentences. Not all the sentences begin with the imperative verb.

- **a** Divide your hair into two even sections and brush it well.
- **b** Illustrate your story with colourful images.
- **c** Present your completed project to your teacher and classmates.
- **d** Download the file to your computer and save it to the desktop.
- **e** Next stir the liquid into the dry ingredients.
- **f** Being careful not to cut yourself, slice the onions finely with a sharp knife.

Sometimes the verb does not come at the beginning of the sentence because the writer needs to add extra information about the action before it is introduced. This extra information might take the form of an **adverbial phrase** or an **adverbial clause**. An adverbial phrase simply gives more information about a verb—when or how the action occurs. An adverbial phrase does not include a complete verb or subject.

The adverbial phrases have been highlighted in these examples:

With great care, remove the tray from the oven.
Before going inside, wipe your feet on the mat.

Activity 2

Underline the **adverbial phrases** and circle the **imperative verbs** in the sentences below. The first one has been done for you.

- **a** Holding the flask firmly, (pour) in the liquid chemicals.
- **b** While holding the dog steady, pour water onto its fur.
- **c** After brushing well, spit the toothpaste into the sink.
- **d** Before lighting the Bunsen burner, check the gas is working.
- **e** While holding down the command and function keys, press delete.

An adverbial clause provides information about who performs an action as well as how and when it occurs. An adverbial clause includes a **subject** (the person doing the action) and a **complete verb** (the action being done).

The adverbial clauses have been highlighted in these examples:

When the mixture begins to bubble, turn the heat down low.

Whenever the cat scratches its fur, squirt it with water.

Underline the **adverbial clause** and circle the **imperative verbs** in the sentences below. The first one has been done for you.

f Once you have eaten your meal, clear the dishes away.

g After you have swept the floors, prepare the soapy water for mopping.

h While your partner whisks the eggs, check the oven is fully preheated.

i While the cake is in the oven, make the icing.

j After buttering your toast, smear on the Vegemite.

Activity 3

Go back to your planning notes for your procedure about treating a bee sting. Use these notes to construct three **imperative sentences**. These don't need to be in the correct order. Make sure each sentence contains an imperative verb and is written in the present tense.

Don't forget that sometimes you might need to add extra information—an adverbial phrase or clause—before the verb.

a ______________________________

b ______________________________

c ______________________________

Spotlight *on spelling*

Technical words

In your school studies you will need to read and write procedures for technical subjects such as Science, Engineering and Multimedia. These procedures will require you to understand and use **technical words** to describe equipment, substances, and so on.

See **Unit 6** for more information on multi-syllabic words.

Technical words are those typically associated with a particular profession, content area or topic. These technical words can be nouns (e.g. *radioactivity*) or adjectives (e.g. *robust*) but for procedures you will mostly encounter technical verbs (e.g. *hypothesise* or *download*).

Technical words can be tricky to spell because most of them are **multi-syllabic** words—that is, they are longer words. You may find these words both hard to read and hard to spell. In order to give yourself a greater chance of spelling success, you can break multi-syllabic words into smaller parts by sounding them out into their syllables. Remember that each syllable should contain a vowel (*a*, *e*, *i*, *o* and *u*) or a vowel sound (*y*).

For example: radioactivity → ra-di-o-ac-ti-vi-ty.

Other **technical words** include:

- consequence (con-se-quence)
- dissolve (dis-solve)
- deduce (de-duce)
- application (app-li-ca-tion)
- protocol (pro-to-col).

Activity 1

Break the following words into their **syllables**. Make sure each syllable has a vowel or vowel sound. You may like to clap out the syllables before you write the answer.

a perspective ______________________

b presentation ______________________

c processor ______________________

d classification ______________________

e explanation ______________________

f evaluate ______________________

Some **technical words** derive from Greek or Latin words. When writing a procedure you may need to make reference to technical terminology—nouns for equipment and verbs for steps to take. To help master the spelling of these words, it's a good idea to learn some of the common Greek or Latin root words, suffixes and prefixes.

The example below shows how the word *respiration* is composed of three parts—the prefix, root and suffix. All of these parts are derived from Greek or Latin words; the meaning of each is in brackets.

prefix	root	suffix
re (back)	*spira* (to breathe)	*tion* (the result of)

The following example shows how a prefix and a suffix can be combined to create a new word. In this case the word is *mutation*.

prefix	suffix
muta (to change)	*tion* (the result of)

Greek/Latin prefixes and their English meanings:

- *anti* (against)
- *un* (not)
- *hemi* (half)
- *philo* (friend/love of)
- *proto* (first).

Greek/Latin suffixes and their English meanings:

- *acro* (height)
- *phobia* (fear).

Greek/Latin root words and their English meanings:

- *hydro* (water)
- *sophy* (wisdom).

Activity 2

Test your knowledge of **scientific** or **technical words** with Greek and Latin origins. Try to identify at least one word beginning or ending with the Greek or Latin **prefixes** or **suffixes** listed below. The first one has been done for you.

a tele (far/distant) teleport, telephone, television

b micro (small) ______

c bi (two) ______

d ology (study of) ______

e psych (mind) ______

f hyper (over) ______

g post (after) ______

h inter (between) ______

You be the teacher

Below are some of the steps for a **procedure** to wash a dog, written by a Year 7 student. There are some errors in the structure of the **steps** and the spelling of some of the **technical words**. Rewrite the series of steps so they are in the correct order and make sure you use the **correct spelling of all words**.

1 After you have given the dog a good wash with shampoo, rinse its fur with water until all suds are removed.

2 First, wash the dog's face.

3 Wash under the dog's legs.

4 Be careful not to get shampoo into its eyes as they are very sensitive.

5 Make sure you check for parrasites like ticks when you do this.

6 Finally, when you've washed the dog you can let it shake its fur to remove exess water.

Now you write

It is now time for you to complete your own **procedure** on treating a bee sting.

1 Before you write, take some time to look at the student writing samples on the following pages as a guide to writing standards. Note the mistakes made in the Intermediate sample and try to avoid making these mistakes yourself.

2 Once you have read the two student writing samples, take some time to think about what you believe are the most important features of a procedure that you need to master. Use the lines below to jot down your answer to this question:

What do you find most difficult when writing this kind of text?

3 Now look at the informative text marking criteria on page viii to double-check that you understand the requirements for a really good piece of informative writing.

Remember that you have already done your planning and drafted your overview, equipment and steps. Use the lines below or your own paper. Good luck!

Looking at other students' writing

Procedures:
What is the procedure for washing a dog?

Introduction
The introduction alerts the audience to the procedure being outlined in the overview.

Informative techniques
The student uses clear and precise language. Second-person point of view is used to instruct the reader through the process of the task.

Text structure
The student uses the correct structure for a procedure: overview, equipment and steps.

Paragraphing
The overview paragraph focuses solely on the reason for the procedure and relevant safety issues.

Cohesion
The focus of the text (how to wash a dog) is sustained throughout. The steps are numbered to help the reader.

ADVANCED SAMPLE

WASHING A DOG

Overview:

It is important to know how to wash a dog as it is a task that should be done routinely as a good pet owner. Before washing your dog you should change into old clothes because dog washing can get messy! Always be sure that your dog is calm and confident before you wash it because scared dogs can quickly become aggressive.

Equipment:

- 1 dog bath or large tub
- 1 bottle of dog shampoo
- 1 dog brush
- 2 towels—one on the floor near the tub
- dog treats

Steps:

1 Half-fill the dog bath or large tub with lukewarm water. Be sure to test that the water is not too hot or too cold!
2 Lift your dog into the water. When coaxing your dog into the bath, try not to splash him with water; dogs don't like this and it may result in a big mess.
3 Use a bucket or another water vessel to soak his coat, making it easier to start shampooing. Keep water away from his ears and face.
4 Using the quantity suggested on your shampoo bottle, pour the shampoo onto your dog's fur.
5 Massage the shampoo into your dog's fur to create a rich lather. Note: if your dog has long hair you may need to use extra shampoo to work it into a lather.
6 Avoid scratching your dog's skin as you lather him up! A light massage or rub would make the bath experience much more enjoyable.
7 Wash under your dog's legs. Make sure you check for parasites like ticks when you do this.
8 Rinse your dog's fur by using the same bucket or vessel you used to soak his hair in step 3. Take care that the soap suds don't run onto his face and ears and make sure that all shampoo residue is gone.
9 Once rinsed, place your dog on the floor towel.
10 Use the other towel to rub your dog dry. It is natural for a dog to want to shake dry, so try and absorb as much water as you can before this happens.

Vocabulary
The student uses appropriate language. Some technical vocabulary is used (e.g. *lukewarm* and *vessel*). Verbs are written in the imperative mood (e.g. *brush* and *massage*).

Sentence structure
The student uses a variety of simple, compound and complex sentences. Imperative sentences are used in the *Steps* section.

Ideas
Each step is detailed and explained clearly.

Punctuation
Complex punctuation is used correctly.

Spelling
All words are spelt correctly, including technical and complex words.

Procedures: *What is the procedure for washing a dog?*

Introduction
The introduction alerts the audience to the procedure being outlined in the first sentence. The student needs to grab the reader's attention with more detail.

Sentence structure
The student uses a variety of simple and compound sentences. but needs to include more complex sentences that demonstrate a better control of language.

INTERMEDIATE SAMPLE

WHAT IS THE PROCEDURE FOR WASHING A DOG?

Overview:

All dog owners should know how to wash their dog. Wear old clothes otherwise you'll get wet. I think you should keep your dog calm because it might bite you.

Equipment:

- 1 dog bath
- some dog shampoo
- 1 dog brush
- some towels—one on the floor near the tub
- maybe dog treats

Steps:

1 Half-fill the dog bath or large tub with water.
2 The dog goes into the water. Dogs don't like this and it may result in a big mess.
3 Use a bucket or something to wet his coat. keeping water away from his ears and face.
4 The quantity suggested on your shampoo bottle, pour the shampoo onto your dog's fur.
5 Massage the shampoo into my dog's fur to create a rich laver.
6 Don't scratch your dog's skin as you lather him up! A light massage or rub would make the bath experience much more enjoyable.
7 You might want to wash under your dog's legs. Make sure you check for ticks when you do this.
8 Rinse your dog's fur by using the same bucket or vessal you used to soak his hair in step 3.
9 Once rinsed, place your dog on the floor towel.
10 Use the other towel to rub your dog dry. They might shake
11 Brush your dog's washed coat to remove hair.

Ideas
The student's ideas are relevant to the procedure. The steps need more detail.

Informative techniques
The student uses mostly clear and precise language. There are occasional errors with the second-person point of view (e.g. *I think* instead of *ensure that* and *my dog's fur* instead of *your dog's fur*).

Punctuation
Simple punctuation is mostly used correctly but there is some missing punctuation (e.g. missing capital letters and misuse of semicolon).

Paragraphing
The overview paragraph focuses on the reason for the procedure and safety issues, but requires more detail.

Spelling
Most words are spelt correctly. There are occasional spelling errors (e.g. 'vessal' for *vessel* and 'laver' for *lather*).

Cohesion
The steps are numbered to help the reader.

Text structure
The student uses the correct structure for a procedure, including an overview, equipment required and relevant steps. They need to include more specific information in the *Equipment* section.

Vocabulary
The student's language is mostly appropriate. More complex vocabulary is needed (e.g. *bite you* for *aggressive*).

The student could use better imperative verbs in steps (e.g. *place the dog* instead of *the dog goes*).

Sentence structure
The student uses a variety of simple and compound sentences. Imperative sentences in the *Steps* section need to begin with imperative verbs (e.g. step 4).

Note: words shaded in blue are errors.

6

UNIT SIX

Informative texts
Research reports

Understanding the question

Investigate a topic relating to young people and music.
Write a report to document your research and findings.

Type of question

This question is asking you to write a particular type of information text—a **research report**.

The word *investigate* suggests that you will need to find out more about the topic—young people and music. The question indicates that you only need to focus on one idea about the topic. This means you need to decide on an aspect of it that interests you by developing your own research question.

Features of a research report

- Aims to answer a question about a particular topic based on information gathered
- Information in the report is organised under headings
- The report is divided into separate sections: aim, method, results, discussion
- Paragraphs are used under each heading
- Language is factual and objective with few personal pronouns
- Passive voice is used to focus on the information rather than the people involved

1 What does the word *investigate* mean? ______________________________

____

2 What does the word *document* mean? ______________________________

____

3 What are the four **content words** in this question?

a ______________________________

b ______________________________

c ______________________________

d ______________________________

4 What does the word *research* mean? ______________________________

____

5 What does the word *report* mean? ______

______

6 What different types of reports can you think of? ______

______

______

______

It takes a very large amount of research before a researcher begins to write a report. Make sure you spend enough time gathering your information and planning before you put pen to paper!

Planning and organisation

Careful **planning** and **organising** of a research report is important if your report is to be accurate and comprehensive.

Asking the right question

All research reports are driven by an **inquiry question** relating to the topic of the report. It is up to you in this task to develop your own question.

The research question you decide to answer must be **open ended**—these are questions with many possible answers. Your question might have one of the following beginnings:

How do/does …? Why do/does …? How should …? Who is/are …?
How might …? What would happen if …?

You should **avoid closed questions** as your research question. These are questions that can simply be answered with yes or no.

For example:

- a closed question is one like *Is rock music bad for you?*
- an open-ended question is one like *How might rock music be bad for young people?*

Identify if the following are **open** or **closed questions**.

a Can fish fly? ______

b Why might some young people dislike school? ______

c What would happen if all politicians were teenagers? ______

d Why do dogs fetch sticks and cats don't? ______

e Is October the month before November? ______

One method that might help you to develop your research question is the **Question Formulation Technique** (**QFT**). It has three steps.

- **Read** the prompt for your research (e.g. young people and music).
- **Write** a list of as many questions as you can think of about that prompt.
- **Identify** which questions are open ended and which are closed.

Activity 2

Follow the **QFT** steps above to develop your own open-ended **research question** for the young people and music topic.

For example: Why do people enjoy video games more when they win?

Research methods

There are a couple of different **research methods** that you could use to get information for your report: surveys and internet/library research. Here we will focus on surveys.

Activity 3

a Write five **survey questions** relating to your research question. For surveys you can use closed questions that require simple answers such as *yes/no/maybe* or *strongly agree/disagree/somewhat agree*.

For example:
Do you listen to rock music? yes/no
I am happiest when I am listening to pop music. agree/disagree/somewhat agree

b Ask up to ten of your friends to complete your **survey**.

It's important to record the ages of participants as you will include this is the method section of your report.

c Look at the **survey** responses carefully and ask yourself these questions:

- What is surprising about the responses? Why?
- What isn't surprising about the responses? Why?
- How do the responses help me answer my research question?
- How do the responses relate to the research topic of young people and music?

You will use your answers to these questions soon when you begin writing your research report.

Structure

A **research report** has a very specific **structure**. It has four sections: **aim**, **method**, **results** and **discussion**. This structure helps your reader follow the process of your research and understand how you reached your findings.

Aim

The **aim** is a brief overview (two to three sentences) of the **purpose** of your research report. It includes the research question.

For example: The aim of this research is to discover which video games young people prefer to play the most.

Activity 1

Write the **aim** of your research report, relating to the topic of young people and music.

Method

This is a short paragraph summarising the **method** of research that you used to gather data for the report. A good method will include the:

- specific **number of subjects** involved (e.g. The survey had 145 respondents.)
- specific details about the **subjects involved** (e.g. Participants were all students at Sydney metropolitan high schools.)
- specific details about the **research method** used (e.g. survey, interview, observation).

For example: A total of twenty young people between the ages of 10 and 14 were asked to complete a ten-question survey about video games. The questions related to video game and console preferences. Just under half of the participants (40%) were female. All participants were asked the same questions.

Activity 2

Match the research question with the most appropriate **method** below. The first one has been done for you.

Question	Method
What effect does violence in the media have on teen crime?	internet/library research
What are Shakespeare's most common character types?	interviews
What impact does global warming have on our environment and our health?	internet/library research
Why do the elderly enjoy gardening?	survey
Who are our community's biggest polluters?	survey

Activity 3

Below are two **method** paragraphs written by Year 8 students. Identify which paragraph is better and provide three reasons why.

a There were some questions that the participants answered. There was something like twenty people who answered the questions, maybe more. They answered a whole range of questions on different topics but mostly about soccer. We observed some people playing soccer as well.

b A total of 100 young people between the ages of 8 and 23 participated in this study. Participants answered twenty-five questions relating to playing soccer in weekend competitions. The survey questions related to the participants' enjoyment of soccer, the time they spend training and the relationships they've developed as a result of playing weekend soccer.

1 ______________________________

____

2 ______________________________

____

3 ______________________________

____

Activity 4

Write a short paragraph summarising the **method** for your research report on young people and music.

____

____

____

____

Results

This is where you provide your readers with an insight into what you discovered from your research (i.e. your **results**). This is usually two or three paragraphs. Order the results from the most important finding to the least important finding.

For example:

Overall, the most frequent response to the survey questions related to new release video games and consoles. Seventy per cent of the participants said that their preference for video games was influenced by the latest releases from popular game developers.

The most popular game developer for both boys and girls was Microsoft Game Developers followed by Mojang. The most popular video game choice was the Halo series with 12/20 participants selecting it. The next most popular choice was Minecraft with 6/20 participants selecting it as their favourite video game.

Activity 5

Below is a summary of **results** from a research project. Rank them in order from most important to least important (1 to 4). The research question is: What chocolate do people prefer to eat?

a ____________ 5% of participants didn't like chocolate at all

b ____________ 60% of participants preferred milk chocolate

c ____________ 30% of participants preferred to eat dark chocolate

d ____________ 10% of participants preferred to eat white chocolate

Activity 6

Go back to the **results** for your survey completed earlier. Write one of the results paragraphs for your research report on young people and music.

____

____

____

Discussion

The **discussion** is usually one or two paragraphs where you discuss what you think your findings mean and **draw conclusions** about the topic. In these paragraphs you make informed guesses about why your research got the results it did. The language must be precise and non-personal, and all opinions must be based on **evidence** from your research.

> For example: The results of the survey were not surprising. The majority of the young people surveyed preferred to play the latest release video games, probably because these are marketed to them by the leading game developers. Overall, the responses demonstrate that the preferences of young gamers are significantly influenced by the latest trends in gaming.

Activity 7

Circle which of these two **discussion paragraphs** you believe is better. Write a brief explanation of your choice.

a There were some weird responses during the interviews and this was interesting. We found it funny that the residents at the nursing home preferred to watch television rather than meet with their families. But they didn't think there was enough channels to choose from. Despite being old, the interviewees were happy to talk to us for hours. We think old people are great.

b The data gathered from the interviews was varied but revealed quite a lot about the recreational habits of the elderly in nursing homes. Many of the interviewees commented that they particularly enjoyed watching the television, however there were frequent complaints about the number of channels available to them. The interviews revealed that these elderly citizens are just as likely to enjoy television as others and therefore their interests should be considered by those in charge of their care.

____

____

____

Activity 8

Match the sentences from the **discussion** sections of reports (on the right) with the aims (on the left). The first one has been done for you.

Aim	Discussion
a To measure the amount of non-recyclable rubbish in local primary schools.	The non-name detergent is considered lesser quality and less likely to be used.
b To discover which brand of detergent is most popular between two varieties.	Sun safety commercials have a significant effect on younger children aged 5 to 10.
c To determine the influence that sun-safety commercials have on children aged 5 to 10.	Primary schools discard far too much non-recyclable rubbish.
d To discover the impact that moving house has on teenagers.	People can track up to four objects moving at moderate speed at any one time.
e To determine if soft drink or fruit juice is more popular with young men aged 18 to 30.	Moving house is a traumatic experience for teenagers.
f To determine how many objects a person can track at one time.	Young men aged 18 to 30 are almost five times more likely to drink soft drink.

Activity 9

In which section of a research report would you put the sentences below? Remember that the sections are: aim, method, results and discussion.

a The results of this experiment will be both encouraging and surprising for parents of teenagers.

b A total of 50 secondary students between the ages of 13 and 17 were asked a series of ten questions relating to their musical preferences.

c Overall, most survey respondents reported that soccer was their favourite sport.

d The purpose of this study is to measure the weight and height of premature babies six months after birth.

e All subjects were male and all were asked the same questions.

Language feature

Active and passive voice

See **Unit 8** on page 87 for more information on **objective** and **subjective voice**.

Research reports are written to **inform**. The language of research reports is factual and objective. In order to create this factual tone, this text type is written using the **passive voice**.

Research reports focus mostly on the information gained from the research and less on the people participating in the research. In order to express this focus, research reports are written in the **passive voice** and not the active voice.

Active voice is when the subject does the action indicated by the verb.

For example:
All participants completed a survey.
subject = participants, object = survey, verb = completed

Smoking causes lung cancer.
subject = smoking, object = cancer, verb = causes

Passive voice is when the object receives the action of the verb

For example:
A survey was completed by all participants.
subject = a survey, object = all participants, verb = were completed

Lung cancer is caused by smoking.
subject = lung cancer, object = smoking, verb = is caused

Activity 1

Identify if these sentences are written using the **active** (A) or **passive** (P) **voice**.

a We believe the mutation causes cancer. __________

b We sequenced the DNA. __________

c The observations were conducted early in the day. __________

d The survey was completed by 40 students. __________

e Twenty couples participated in the experiment. __________

f The cells were categorised by the scientists. __________

Activity 2

Rewrite these sentences from **active** to **passive voice**. The first one has been done for you.

a Researchers tested the 300 subjects.

The 300 subjects were tested by the researchers.

b The researchers collected the data over three weeks.

____

c The students counted the rubbish.

____

d The young men preferred soft drink.

____

e The children watched the commercials three times.

____

f Teenagers don't enjoy moving house.

____

More multi-syllabic words

As you learnt in Unit 5, the words that we most frequently misspell are the longer words. These words are difficult because there are so many letters—it's easy to get confused and get something incorrect!

Multi-syllabic words appear frequently in research reports because these reports are often written about technical or scientific topics. (You can read more about technical words in Unit 5.)

Sometimes multi-syllabic words are made up of three parts—the root word, a suffix and a prefix. Remember that sometimes the spelling of the root word changes when adding a suffix. Check Units 9 and 10 to refresh your knowledge of these.

Activity 1

Add a suffix and a prefix from the list in the table to the words in the table to create **multi-syllabic words**. Cross off prefixes/suffixes as you use them. Remember that for words ending with *e* drop the *e* before adding the suffix. The first one has been done for you.

Prefix	Suffix
de	*able*
un	*ible*
in	*ing*
un	*ition*
de	*ingly*
de	*ed*

a believe unbelievable

b surprise ____________________

c access ____________________

d grade ____________________

e compose ____________________

f stabilise ____________________

Remember that sometimes **multi-syllabic words** just have a long root word and a suffix or prefix.

Sometimes **multi-syllabic words** are just long words. In this case, it helps to break the word into smaller parts by sounding it out into its syllables.

Activity 2

Add a suffix or a prefix from the list in the table to the words below to create **multi-syllabic words**.

Prefix	**Suffix**
ir	*ion*
un	*ion*
trans	*less*

a destitute ______________________

b perfect ______________________

c taste ______________________

d relevant ______________________

e plant ______________________

f finished ______________________

Activity 3

Break the following words into their **syllables**. Remember that each syllable should contain a vowel (*a*, *e*, *i*, *o* and *u*) or a vowel sound (*y*).

a surveying ______________________

b originate ______________________

c investigate ______________________

d interviewees ______________________

e persistent ______________________

f occurrence ______________________

You be the teacher

Below is a **method paragraph** for a blog post written by a Year 7 student. There are some errors in the structure of the paragraph and the spelling of some of the **multi-syllabic words**. Improve the structure and rewrite the paragraph with the **correct spelling of all words**.

All participants were aged between 10 to 14 years. Survey questions related to frequency of gaming, accessbility to gaming consoles and game prefrenccces. Participants were asked a series of ten questions about their use of video games. Ten boys and ten girls were included in this experment. The particpants were randomly selected using a criteria relating to socioeconomic status, age and gender.

Now you write

It is now time for you to complete your own **research report** on young people and music.

1 Before you write, take some time to look at the student writing samples on the following pages as a guide to writing standards. Note the mistakes made in the intermediate sample and try to avoid making these mistakes yourself.

2 Once you have read the two student writing samples, take some time to think about what you believe are the most important features of a research report that you need to master. Use the lines below to jot down your answer to this question:

What do you find most difficult when writing this kind of text?

3 Now look at the informative text marking criteria on page viii to double-check that you understand the requirements for a really good piece of informative writing.

Remember that you have already done your planning and drafted your aim, method, results and discussion. Use your own paper. Good luck!

Looking at other students' writing

Investigate a topic relating to young people and video games.
Write a report to document your research and findings.

Introduction
The student alerts the audience to the aim of the research immediately. The student uses succinct sentences to outline the aim.

Informative techniques
The student uses clear and precise language. Third-person narrative is used to create an objective, factual tone.

Text structure
The student uses the correct structure for a research report, including an aim, method, results and discussion.

Paragraphing
Each paragraph features detailed and appropriate information under report headings.

Cohesion
Each paragraph opens with a succinct topic sentence. All paragraphs focus on the central topic of the report—video games and young people.

ADVANCED SAMPLE

INVESTIGATE A TOPIC RELATING TO YOUNG PEOPLE AND VIDEO GAMES.

Aim:

The aim of this research is to discover which video games and consoles young people prefer to play the most.

Method:

A total of twenty young people between the ages of 10 and 14 were asked to complete a ten-question survey about video games. The questions related to video game and console preferences. Just under half of the participants (40%) were female. All participants were asked the same questions.

Results:

Overall, the most frequent response to the survey questions related to new release video games and consoles. Seventy per cent of the participants said that their preference for video games was influenced by the latest releases from popular game developers. The most popular game developer for both boys and girls was Microsoft Game Developers followed by Mojang. The most popular video game choice was the Halo series with 12/20 participants selecting it. The next most popular choice was Minecraft with 6/20 participants selecting it as their favourite video game.

Discussion:

The results of the survey were not surprising. The majority of the young people surveyed preferred to play the latest release video games, probably because these are marketed to them by the leading game developers. Overall, the responses demonstrate that the preferences of young gamers are significantly influenced by the latest trends in gaming.

Vocabulary
The language used is appropriate. Complex vocabulary is used and appropriate to a research report (e.g. *participants* and *responses*).

Sentence structure
The student uses a variety of simple, compound and complex sentences.

Ideas
Strong ideas that are relevant to the topic are included in each body paragraph. Ideas are detailed and well explained.

Punctuation
The student uses complex punctuation correctly.

Spelling
All words are spelt correctly, including technical and complex words.

Investigate a topic relating to young people and video games.

Write a report to document your research and findings.

Introduction
The student alerts the audience to the topic in the first sentence. The student needs to better outline the specific focus of the research.

Sentence structure
The student uses a variety of simple and compound sentences but needs to include complex sentences to explain more complex ideas.

INTERMEDIATE SAMPLE

INVESTIGATE A TOPIC RELATING TO YOUNG PEOPLE AND VIDEO GAMES.

Aim:

The aim of this research is to find out information about young people and gaming.

Method:

A group of young people were asked to complete our survey about video games. I think the questions were about what video game; and consoles those kids preferred. Just under half of the kids were girls. All kids got the same questions.

Results:

It looks like most of the kids wanted to give answers about new consoles and new video games. Something like 70% of them said that they really liked games by popular game developpers because they are cool. Boys and girls both were stoked on microsoft Game Developers followed by mojang. The most popular video game was the Halo series and the next most popular choice was Minecraft.

Discussion:

The results of the survey tell a lot. Most young people surveyed liked to play the latest release video games, probably because the leading game developers market these to them. Overall, the responses show that the choices of young gamers are influencced by the latest trends in gaming.

Ideas
The student uses good ideas that are relevant to the topic. Some ideas need more detail.

Informative techniques
The student uses some vague and imprecise language (e.g. *something like*, *probably because* and *I think the questions …*). There are occasional errors with the third person (e.g. 'our survey' instead of 'a survey').

Punctuation
Simple punctuation is mostly correct but there is some missing punctuation (e.g. missing capital letters and misuse of a semicolon).

Paragraphing
Each paragraph features a basic reason relevant to the heading. The paragraphs need more detail to support the ideas.

Spelling
Most words are spelt correctly. There are occasional spelling errors with multi-syllabic words (e.g. 'developpers' for *developers* and 'influencced' for *influenced*).

Cohesion
Each paragraph opens with a basic sentence.

Text structure
The student uses the correct structure for a research report, featuring the aim, method, results and discussion but needs to include stronger opening sentences for each paragraph.

Vocabulary
The language used is mostly appropriate. More complex vocabulary is needed (e.g. *participants* for *kids*, *preference* for *really liked*).

The student should avoid colloquial language such as *stoked*.

Note: words shaded in blue are errors.

UNIT SEVEN

Informative texts
Explanatory essays

Understanding the question

Write an essay explaining the following topic:
How can children help out at home?

Type of question

You are required to write an **explanatory essay** in response to a specific question. The word *explain* is the clue to what type of essay you should write. You are not being asked to present your personal opinion on the topic—you are being asked to explain the topic to your reader.

You must develop a structured response that helps your reader better understand the focus of the question: how children help out at home.

Remember that the purpose of this essay type is to **educate your reader**.

Features of an explanatory essay

- Aims to explain a topic to the reader
- Has a strong structure: introduction, body and conclusion
- Paragraphs are sequenced to make a smooth transition between ideas about the topic
- Language is clear and precise to help the reader understand the topic
- Abstract nouns are often included to explain the issues (e.g. *commitment*)
- Language is mostly factual and free from bias or opinion

1 The question above includes one key **task word** that tells you what you need to do in this piece of writing. In your own words, write a brief definition of it.

Look back at **Unit 2** to find out about **task words**.

____

____

____

____

2 Identify the **task words** in the questions below.

a Explain why children should go to school. ______________

b Discuss the consequences of not showering for a year. ______________

c Argue why students should be allowed to use mobile phones in class. ______________

Planning and organisation

Why is planning important for this form of essay? The purpose of an explanatory essay is to help your reader **clearly understand a topic**—that means you must plan carefully to ensure you achieve this goal!

Brainstorm

The first step before writing any essay is to **brainstorm**. The best method to help start brainstorming is a spider-map.

Activity 1

On the spider-map below, add all of the things children can do to help around the house (e.g. they may do the washing-up every evening after dinner).

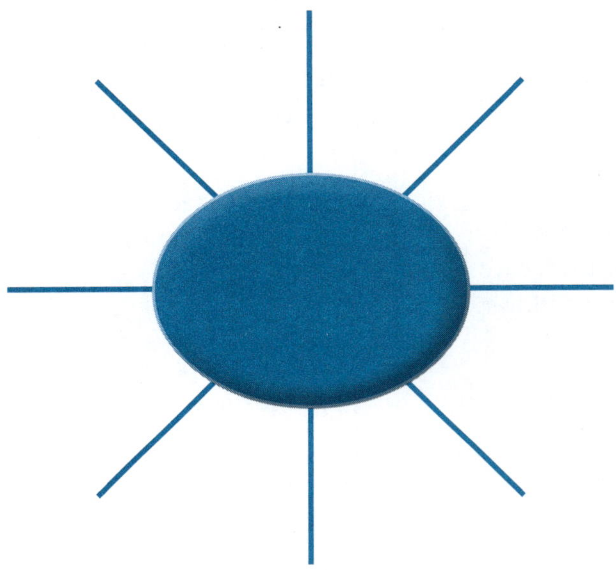

Look back at **Unit 1** to find out about **spider-maps**.

Selection of ideas

From your brainstorm above, **select** three activities that children can do to help around the house (e.g. wash-up, clean their room and fold the washing).

These activities will form the basis of your explanatory essay. You can help develop these ideas further using a mind-map. A mind-map is a more detailed form of brainstorming tool than a spider-map.

Look at the example given below for the topic *Cats*. See how lines have been used to show the relationship between ideas?

Activity 2

What do you think the explanatory **essay topic** was for the mind-map below?

a Write an essay explaining why cats make good pets.

b Write an essay explaining the differences between cats.

c Write an essay explaining why feral cats are bad for the environment.

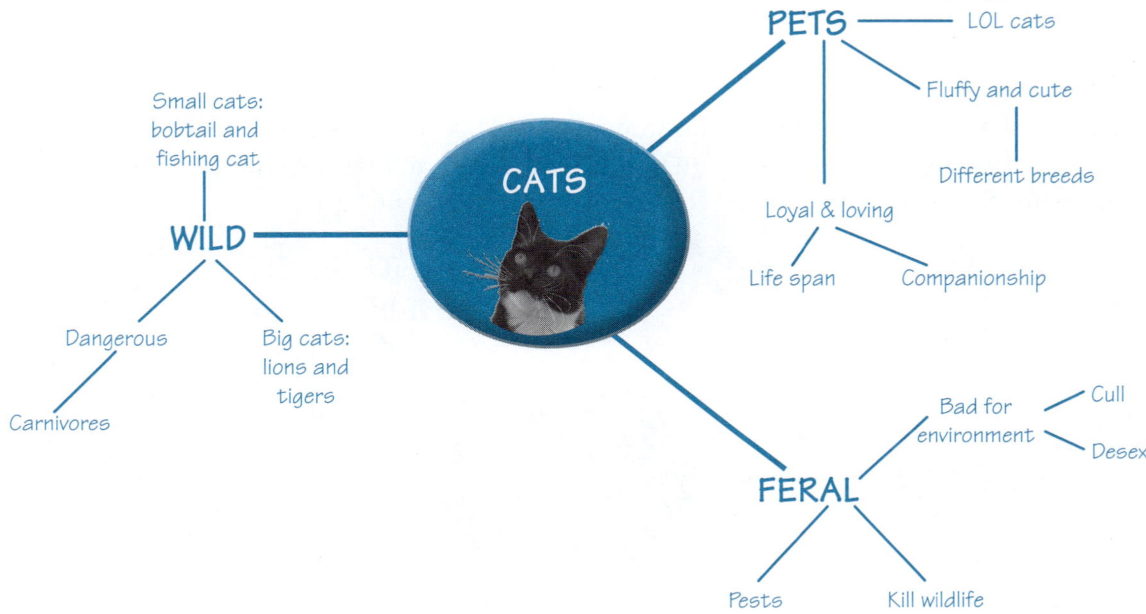

Activity 3

Use your own paper to create a mind-map with the **topic** of *Activities children can do to help around the house*. Remember to only focus on the three activities you selected from the spider-map.

You might want to include:

- a name/brief description of the activity
- how often they might do the activity
- how difficult the activity is
- who helps them with the activity
- if they should get pocket money for doing the activity
- if they would/wouldn't enjoy the activity
- the steps involved in completing the activity.

This information will form the basis of the paragraphs for your explanatory essay.

Structure

Explanatory essays follow this structure: **introductory** paragraph, **body** paragraphs and **concluding** paragraph.

Introductory paragraph

The first paragraph of your explanatory essay is designed to introduce your reader to the topic of your essay. Usually in the **introduction** to an explanatory essay you will provide a **brief outline** of the topic and try to **interest your reader** so they will continue to read the rest of your essay.

Activity 1

Look at the mind-map below that a student created in response to the question *Why are parents so strict?* Use the information to write an **introduction** to their explanatory essay. Remember to briefly refer to all three main reasons identified by the student.

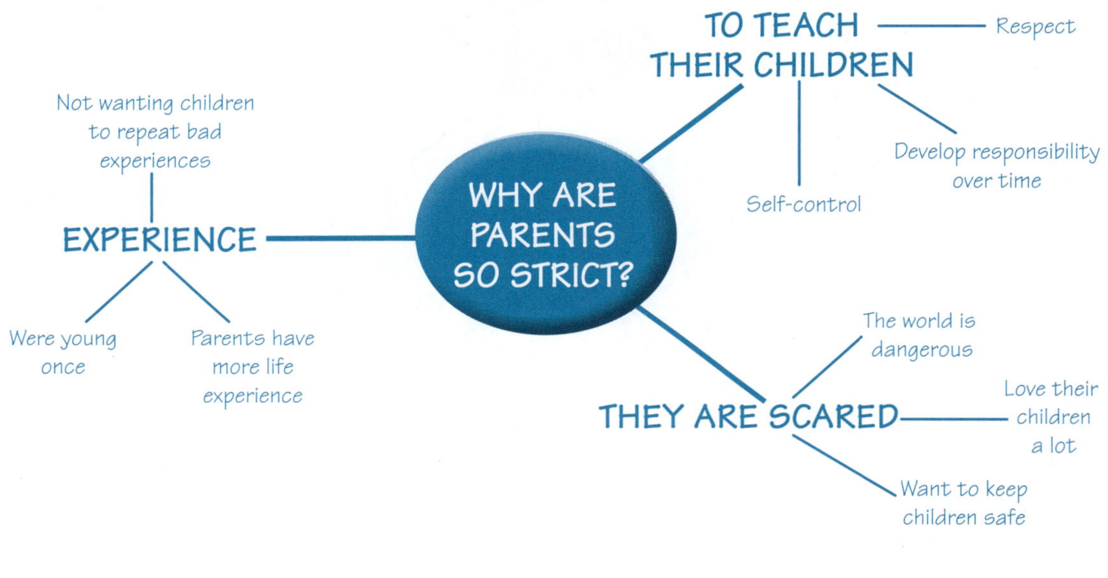

Activity 2

Now try to write the **introduction** for your explanatory essay topic.

Body paragraphs

The **body** of your explanatory essay is made up of a sequence of paragraphs. The purpose of the essay body is to **explain the topic** in depth. Each paragraph explains a separate aspect of the topic being explained in your essay. Each paragraph will begin with a **topic sentence** and will provide **supporting evidence** to support this topic sentence.

A topic sentence briefly **summarises the topic** that will be the focus for the paragraph. Topic sentences often feature one important noun. Often this noun comes at the very beginning of the sentence.

For example: **Deforestation** is the process of cutting down and clearing forests of trees.

In the example above, the noun is *deforestation*. By placing this important noun at the beginning of the topic sentence, the reader knows what the focus of that paragraph will be—deforestation!

Now look at the whole paragraph on deforestation.

Deforestation is the process of cutting down and clearing forests of trees. One of the most common reasons for deforestation is the need to clear land for farming purposes. Farmers often cut down trees and then grind the stumps. These trees may be sold for fuel and the ground-up stumps used for mulch.

Activity 3

In the **topic sentences** below, underline the important noun(s) that indicate the topic of the paragraph. The first one has been done for you.

- **a** There are many possible contributing factors to global warming.
- **b** There are many reasons why pollution in ABC Town is the worst in the world.
- **c** There are a number of steps to be taken when fixing a bicycle tyre.
- **d** There are several advantages to growing up in a small town.
- **e** Another important resource for student success is frequent use of the library.

Concluding paragraph

The **final paragraph** of your explanatory essay is called the conclusion. The purpose of the conclusion is to **summarise your main points** and **remind your reader** about what they have just read. Your final statement will remind the reader that this is an important topic to understand fully.

Activity 4

Look at the two **conclusions** on the next page. Both are conclusions for an essay explaining why parents are so strict. Circle the best conclusion from the two—remember that the conclusion for an explanatory essay will be clear and definite and **capture the main points** discussed without going over them again. A conclusion shouldn't introduce any new ideas not discussed previously in the body of the essay.

Conclusion one

It is difficult to explain all of the motives for why parents are so strict. However, there are a few main reasons. These are fear for the safety and wellbeing of their children, their own previous experiences of being young and the desire to educate their children about respect and self-control. It is important that children clearly understand the reasons behind their parents' rules and expectations.

Conclusion two

It is difficult to explain all of the motives for why parents are so strict. Sometimes parents are just being unfair because they had a tough childhood. Other reasons include parents being over-protective and not wanting their children to be bored at terrible parties. Mostly we don't know why parents are so strict, maybe they are just mean.

Activity 5

Now have a go at writing the **conclusion** for your explanatory essay topic.

Language feature

Third-person narrative

Most essays that you write will be written in the **third person**. The third person is the use of the pronouns *he*, *she* and *they*; it avoids the use of the first-person pronouns *I*, *we* and *us*. Explanatory essays are usually **objective** and **free of bias** and to achieve this you should avoid writing from the first-person point of view—this means you shouldn't use the personal pronoun *I*. Instead you should write from the third-person point of view.

Common words writers use to avoid being too personal are:

* Many people ...
* It is common ...
* It has been concluded that ...
* This may result from ...

For example:

First person: I think that helping your parents around the house teaches responsibility.

Third person: Helping parents around the house teaches young people responsibility.

Activity 1

Change the following sentence from the first person to the **third person**.

a I enjoyed helping my parents because it means they are less stressed and can spend more time with me.

b I think parents are strict because they care a lot about their children.

c I do a lot of jobs around the house to help my parents; for example, I mow the lawn once a week.

d My parents pay me ten dollars a week to help them around the house.

e I always make sure I pack away my things immediately after I have finished using them.

Spotlight *on spelling*

Nominalisation

Nouns in explanatory essays are often abstract nouns. An **abstract noun** is something you can't see but something you can feel, experience or think about such as love, help or responsibility.

Many abstract nouns are formed by **nominalisation**—this is simply changing a verb into a noun. Nominalisation is important because it allows us to **focus on actions** (verbs) as things (nouns). This means we can better explain the 'thing' to our readers.

For example: Helping around the house is easier if you **organise** (verb) your time well.
Organisation (noun) of your time can make helping around the house easier.

See how in the example above the focus has shifted from *helping* to *organisation* by changing the verb *organise* to the noun *organisation*. This tells the reader that the focus of the paragraph will be on organisation.

Nominalisation can make your writing more sophisticated, but don't overdo it! Only use them if you feel ready to—it is better to write using language you understand because then your writing will be clearer.

Activity 1

Match the **verb** to its correct **suffix**. The first one has been done for you.
Note: Most will not require spelling changes to the end of the original word but some will, so keep an eye out!

a	amuse	tion
b	abduct	ment
c	evict	ism
d	advance	ion
e	command	ment
f	terror	ness
g	criticise	ism
h	evident	tion
i	relate	ce
j	happy	ment

Activity 2

Below is a list of verbs. **Nominalise** each verb by adding its correct suffix. Most will not require spelling changes to the end of the original word but some will, so look out for these!

Verb	**Noun**
equip	
refresh	
involve	
develop	
infect	
connect	

You be the teacher

Below is a **body paragraph** for an explanatory essay written by a Year 8 student. There are some errors in the structure of the paragraph and the spelling of some of the **nominalisations**. There is also one unnecessary sentence that needs to be removed. Rewrite the paragraph with the **correct spelling of all words**. Remember that an explanatory essay begins with a clear **topic sentence!**

Washing up takes no longer than twenty minutes and can be made quicker if someone else does the drying up. Organisattion and care is required during this activity, as there is the potentshal to break crockery. I once broke a cup when I was doing the washing up. Assistence with washing up after dinner is just one way that children can help their parents out at home. Children should do the washing up every night after dinner because this helps their parents a lot.

Now you write

It is now time for you to complete your own **explanatory essay** on the *Helping out at home* topic.

1 Before you write, take some time to look at the student writing samples on the following pages as a guide to writing standards. Note the mistakes made in the Intermediate sample and try to avoid making these mistakes yourself.

2 Once you have read the two student writing samples, take some time to think about what you believe are the most important features of an explanatory essay that you need to master. Use the lines below to jot down your answer to this question:

What do you find most difficult when writing this kind of text?

3 Now look at the informative text marking criteria on page viii to double-check that you understand the requirements for a really good piece of informative writing.

Remember that you have already done your planning and drafted your introduction, conclusion and one body paragraph. Use your own paper. Good luck!

Looking at other students' writing

Explanatory essays:

Write an essay explaining why parents are so strict.

Introduction
The student alerts the audience to the topic in the first sentence with a complex sentence. A brief outline of the topic is given.

Informative techniques
The student uses clear and precise language. Third-person narrative is used to create an objective, factual tone.

Text structure
The student uses the correct structure for an explanatory essay, including an introduction, a body and a conclusion. The topic sentences are effective.

Paragraphing
Each paragraph features one thoughtful and detailed explanation of a central idea.

Cohesion
Each paragraph opens with a topic sentence. Connectives are used to introduce each new idea (e.g. *another* and *finally*).

ADVANCED SAMPLE

WRITE AN ESSAY EXPLAINING WHY PARENTS ARE SO STRICT.

Children and teenagers sometimes feel that their parents are too strict. However, there are reasons for parents being strict. One of the more common explanations for this is because parents are scared for the safety of their children. Another reason is that they wish to educate their children about respect and self-control. Finally, parents may be strict simply because they have more life experience.

Concern for the safety of their children is one reason parents are strict. Sometimes children forget that parents are human beings with feelings too. Parents devote their lives to the safety and wellbeing of their children and often they use a series of rules to protect their children from harm. The world can be quite a dangerous place and parents seek to protect their children from these dangers. The decisions made by parents to protect their children may seem unfair.

The education of their children about the importance of respect is another reason why parents may also be strict. Young people often want to control their own lives and feel free to make their own rules. Unfortunately this can result in young people without any self-control. The rules set by parents can also help children to develop respect for others, as they learn to obey rules. What may seem to be strict parents may in fact be a good learning experience for children.

Finally, parents may be strict simply because they have more life experience and have a better understanding of appropriate behaviours. The longer that a person is alive, the more experience they have. Parents have more life experience than children and have a better understanding of acceptable behaviours. Also, parents may have had their own bad experiences as young people and wish to protect their children from making the same mistakes.

It is difficult to explain all of the motives for why parents are strict. However, a few key reasons are fear for the safety of their children, their own previous experiences and the desire to educate their children about respect. It is important that both children and parents clearly understand the reasons behind parents being strict.

Vocabulary
The language used is appropriate. Complex vocabulary is used (e.g. *boundaries, self-control* and *devote*).

Sentence structure
The student uses a variety of simple, compound sentences and complex sentences. Nominalisations are used in topic sentences (e.g. *concern* and *education*).

Ideas
Strong ideas that are relevant to the topic are included in each body paragraph. Ideas are detailed and well explained.

Punctuation
Complex punctuation is used correctly.

Spelling
All words are spelt correctly, including technical and complex words.

Explanatory essays:

Write an essay explaining why parents are so strict.

Introduction
The student alerts the audience to the topic in the first sentence but needs to grab the reader's attention more effectively with a more complex sentence.

Spelling
Most words used are spelt correctly. There are occasional spelling errors (e.g. 'misstakes' for *mistakes* and 'explanattions' for *explanations*). The student needs to use nominalisations more confidently.

Sentence structure
The student uses a variety of simple and compound sentences but needs to include complex sentences to explain more complex ideas. The student uses very few nominalisations.

INTERMEDIATE SAMPLE

WRITE AN ESSAY EXPLAINING WHY PARENTS ARE SO STRICT.

Parents are strict but there are explanattions for this. Some reasons include parents being scared, parents wanting kids to learn to be good and because parents know more about the world.

Parents are scared our children might get hurt. Sometimes children forget that parents are human beings with feelings too. Parents spend their lives keeping their children safe and this is why they make rules. The world can be dangerous and parents don't want their kids getting hurt. Sometimes the rules parents make are too tough.

Parents want their children to learn how to be good. young people like to be free and have no rules. But this might mean children are wild. The rules made by parents can also help children to be better behaved. Having rules can be good for children.

Parents have lived longer and know more about the world. This means parents know more about what can hurt their kids. Parents don't want their kids to make bad misstakes in life.

It is difficult to explain all the reasons why parents are strict but some include wanting to keep kids safe, learning from own experiences and wanting to educate their children. both parents and children need to understand why parents can be strict.

Informative techniques
The student uses mostly clear and precise language. There are occasional errors with the third person (e.g. *our children* instead of *their children*).

Paragraphing
Each paragraph features one basic reason to support the idea being explained. The paragraphs need more detail to support ideas.

Ideas
The student uses good ideas that are relevant to the topic. Their ideas need more detail.

Punctuation
Simple punctuation is mostly correct but there is some missing punctuation (e.g. missing capital letters).

Cohesion
Each paragraph opens with a basic sentence. Connectives should be used to introduce each new idea (e.g. *furthermore*).

Text structure
The student uses the correct structure for an explanatory essay, including an introduction, a body and a conclusion. The student needs to include stronger opening sentences beginning with one important noun.

Vocabulary
The language used is mostly appropriate but there is some informal language (e.g. *kids*). More complex vocabulary is needed (e.g. *devote* for *spend*, *appropriate behaviours* for *being good*).

The student could use better adjectives to provide more information about the world (e.g. *dangerous and challenging*).

Note: words shaded in blue are errors.

Informative texts

News reports

Understanding the question

News reports:
Write a news report about a bank robbery.

Type of question

This question is asking you to write a particular type of informative text—a **news report**.

The purpose of a news report is to **provide readers with the facts** about an event that has happened very recently. News reports provide the what, who, when, why and how of recent events.

News reports differ in important ways from other kinds of reports, such as research reports.

Features of a news report

- Aims to inform people about the latest news
- Headline attracts attention and sums up the content of the report
- First paragraph alerts the reader to the main event of the news story
- Has a series of short paragraphs
- Uses objective, non-biased language
- Uses direct and indirect speech of witnesses or authorities
- Sentences are factual and to the point
- Uses third-person narrative
- Written in past tense

1 Use a dictionary to define these words.

a news ____________________

b report ____________________

2 List five other events for which you may be asked to write a report.

For example: a car accident.

a ____________________

b ____________________

c ____________________

d ____________________

e ____________________

Planning and organisation

This task involves writing a made-up news report about a bank robbery. You will need to use your imagination to create important **content**, specifically the *what, when, where, who, how* and *why* relating to the event. However, try to make the content of your report as believable as possible. You might even like to refer to real people and places.

Activity 1

In the box below, add all that you know about bank robberies. The following are some things you might consider.

- Where does a bank robbery take place?
- When might a robbery take place (what time of day and what day of the week)?
- What type of people are usually involved?
- Why might someone rob a bank?
- How might they get away with it?
- How might the robbers have got into the bank and/or escaped?

Activity 2

Complete the table below to **plan** your news report about a bank robbery.

What is being reported?	
Who was involved?	
When did it happen?	
Why did it happen?	
How did it happen?	
Where did it happen?	

Structure

Fewer people are reading newspapers these days as they are accessing their news online. However, the **structure** and language of the **news reports** written by the bigger news providers has remained mostly the same online and in print: **headline**, **byline**, **introductory** paragraph, **body** paragraphs and **concluding** paragraph.

Headline

Every news report begins with a **headline**. This is a very short statement—sometimes only a few words—that makes the main point of the article clear for readers. The purpose of a headline is to **grab the attention** of the readers.

- Headlines might include a **pun.** A pun is a play on words.
  For example: A report about a lost watch might have a headline *Lost time.*
- Headlines might include **alliteration.** Alliteration is the repetition of consonants at the beginning of words.
  For example: A report about landing on the moon might have a headline *Men make Moon.*
- Headlines might **omit unnecessary words.** Words such as articles and prepositions are often left out of headlines to make them short and more eye-catching.
  For example: A headline would read *Brown Gets Gold* instead of *Brown gets a gold medal in her race.*

Activity 1

Match the **headline** to the story summary.

Report summary	Headline
Local river is polluted by paint factory	Man Saves Best Friend
Car accident in busy shopping mall	Eagles Win Cup
Man saves his dog from drowning in surf	Red River Rage
Football team wins grand final	Car Ploughs Through Mall

Activity 2

Write a **headline** for each of the summarised news stories below. Don't forget to use one of the three features of headlines as outlined above!

a A horse is found wandering on a popular beach. ____________________

b School students celebrate the centenary of their school. ____________________

c A movie star attends a homeless shelter to serve dinner. ____________________

d A giant jellyfish washes up on a crowded beach. ____________________

e Woman gives birth to triplets at local shopping centre. ____________________

Activity 3

Now write the **headline** for your news report on the bank robbery.

____

Byline

Most news reports have a **byline**. This is the **name** of the person who wrote the report. It comes just under the headline and just before the first paragraph of the report. For online news reports the byline includes the date and location of when the report was written.

Introductory paragraph

The **introductory paragraph** tells the reader what the article is about. It contains the **main point** of the news story, usually in a direct, factual and dramatic way. The purpose of this paragraph is to **attract the reader's interest**.

For example: Two teenagers have been charged over the vandalism of a park in Greenville. Local residents witnessed the two boys, aged 14 and 16, as they were leaving the park.

Activity 4

Write the first paragraph for your robbery report.

____

____

____

____

____

Body paragraphs

The **body** of a news report consists of a series of paragraphs that provide the **what**, **who**, **when**, **where**, **why** and **how** of a recent event. The following are key features of body paragraphs.

- One point about the news story is made per paragraph.
- The events of a story are not always reported in the order that they occurred in the 'real world'.
- Paragraphs for news reports do not contain obvious topic sentences.
- Paragraphs are very short—one or two sentences only.
- The vocabulary is simple so everyone can read the news.
- Sentences are short, factual and to the point.
- Most sentences are written in the past tense because the news article is reporting on something that has already happened.
- Evidence from witnesses or authority figures is reported through direct and indirect speech.

Activity 5

Below is a sentence summarising the events reported in a newspaper. For each event, **identify** three people who might be quoted to give evidence to support the story.

1 A house was destroyed during a fire caused by a gas leak with the occupants escaping just minutes before the roof collapsed.

a ______________________________

b ______________________________

c ______________________________

2 A young boy has been reunited with his parents after he was discovered alive and well having been locked in the local Woolworths supermarket for a night.

a ______________________________

b ______________________________

c ______________________________

Activity 6

The following report begins well with a good headline and first paragraph. However, the body paragraphs can be improved. **Correct** this by marking at least two spots where the sentences are too long or complex, or where the paragraphs include more than one point.

Barking mad neighbours

After dealing with the continuous barking of the dogs in their streets, locals in Pitt Street have decided to take actions into their own hands.

The locals have started playing classical music loudly through car speakers and throwing large bones for the dogs to eat but this has enraged some dog owners but some are happy with the moves. The dogs in the street range from small Chihuahuas to a big Rottweiler.

The actions have come as a surprise to the dog owners but one of the owners commented that, 'This was like Christmas for our dogs and we hope it continues.' and another observed that they had not noticed the dogs barking. It seems that the generous response from the dogless won't be ending any time soon.

Concluding paragraph

The purpose of a **concluding paragraph** is to **emphasise** the **main point** of the news report. This paragraph is more than the end of the story because often a news event will continue to be reported over a series of days.

The example paragraph below concludes the news report given earlier in the discussion of paragraph structure.

> The boys will appear in St George Magistrates Court tomorrow. 'It is upsetting that once again we have young people showing a lack of respect for their community,' Constable Trent said.

Activity 7

Which of the paragraphs below works best as a **conclusion** for the report about barking dogs? Circle your choice and use the lines below to give reasons for your answer.

a The neighbours plan to hold a monthly 'Doggy Picnic'. The event is designed to strengthen relationships between humans and canines.

b Every night the neighbours deliver new treats to the dogs in the hopes of keeping them occupied. It seems to be working.

c The local police have reported a decline in the number of complaints about barking dogs in recent months.

Activity 8

Write the **concluding paragraph** for your report on the robbery.

Language feature

Objective language

News reports are written to provide information about current events. The purpose is simply to **inform**, not to persuade. To do this, news reports use only **objective language**.

Objective language is factual, non-biased and impersonal language. Its purpose is to **provide information**. **Subjective language**, on the other hand, is personal and often aims to **evoke emotions** or the **imagination**.

Objective language:

- is written in the third person—this means no personal pronouns like *I, we, us* or *me*
- has very few adjectives or descriptive language
- does not include a personal opinion about the events.

  For example: The man walked into the bar at approximately 7.30 pm and is said to have been armed with a revolver.

Here is an example of **subjective language**:

  The sinister man walked into the dingy bar early in the evening and I've been told by witnesses that he was carrying a scary-looking revolver.

Activity 1

Identify if the following are examples of **subjective** or **objective language**.

Example	Subjective/objective
a His cold voice reminded me of a snake and trembled as he spoke.	
b Witnesses identified the suspect by the tattoos on his neck.	
c Residents reported that the rain stopped mid-morning.	
d I sought refuge from the throbbing thunder under the nearest tree.	

Activity 2

The sentences below are too descriptive for a news report. Rewrite each sentence using **objective language** to make it more suitable for the news report form.

a On a blisteringly hot summer's day the fire raged like a demon through the small town.

b The stern and serious Constable Black cried, 'This is a tragedy for the Bluelake Community.'

c The strange looking Mr Anstley accepted his undeserved award for heroism.

d The badly damaged boat was dragged into the unfriendly harbour by the unhappy coast guards.

Activity 3

The sentences below are too personal for a news report. Rewrite each sentence using **objective language** to make it more suitable for the news report form.

a In Australia there are large penalties for littering and I think this is a good thing.

b At the time of the accident most sensible people were asleep in their beds, like me.

c I think the Sydney 2000 Olympics were good for Australian sport and for our spirit.

d The New Zealand Prime Minister, Helen Clarke, wore a silver skirt and white blouse, a lot like the one my mother owns.

e I can understand why many people in the community don't support the policies of our local government.

Spotlight on spelling

Common confusions and misspellings

When writing a news report it is very important to use correct spelling. News reports shouldn't contain a lot of difficult and complex words because they need to be made accessible to people with a wide range of reading abilities. There are, unfortunately, a few everyday words that are commonly confused or misspelt.

Ending with *ise* or *ice*

There is a little trick that can help you decide if a word should be spelt with *ise* or *ice*. Words with these endings are spelt with an *ise* when they are **verbs** and an *ice* when they are **nouns**. Also, with words like *advise*/*advice* and *devise*/*device* you can hear the difference in sound between *ice* and *ise*.

Activity 1

advice   advise   device   devise   practice   practise   licence   license

Put the words above into the correct columns in the table below. The first one has been done for you.

Noun	Verb
advice	advise

Activity 2

Using the same words from the last activity, write the correct word in the space provided and circle whether it is a **verb** or a **noun**.

a I love to hear my sister ____________ her flute. (noun/verb)

b Liv was delighted when she passed her driver's ____________ test. (noun/verb)

c It was on the ____________ of my English teacher that I entered the writing competition. (noun/verb)

d I still don't know how to work the phone charging ____________ that my son gave me. (noun/verb)

Homophones

Some words **sound alike** but have different spellings and different meanings. These are called **homophones**.

Activity 3

Check your knowledge of these commonly misspelt **homophones** by circling the correct word in each of the following sentences.

- **a** We are very pleased to inform you that (you're/your) now officially a student at Treetop High School.
- **b** The dietician said that (it's/its) Harry's weight that is causing him to sleep badly at night.
- **c** When is (you're/your) mother going to be home?
- **d** Sharon was delighted by (their/they're/there) sudden popularity.
- **e** I didn't know (whether/weather) I would make it to school tomorrow, having sprained my ankle at netball.
- **f** I never know (were/where/wear) my school shoes are in the morning.

More common confusions

These three word pairs are not quite **homophones** but they often cause problems. Have a look at each pair and the explanation of how they are used differently.

- **effect/affect**

  The word *affect* is a verb. It means to influence or change something.

  For example: I was **affected** by the emotional music.

  The word *effect* is a noun. It is the result of something being changed or altered.

  For example: The audience crying was the **effect** the composer desired.

- **loose/lose/loss**

  These three words are very much alike. The word *loose* is an adjective.

  For example: My skirt is very **loose**.

  The word *lose* is a verb.

  For example: I don't want to **lose** my sister.

  The word *loss* is a noun.

  For example: Mary wasn't coping well with the **loss** of her phone.

- **then/than**

  These two words are also very much alike. The word *then* is a connective adverb and indicates a sequence of events.

  For example: She fell over **then** I did too.

  The word *than* is used to indicate comparison between two things.

  For example: I am much heavier **than** he is.

Activity 4

Underline the correct word in each of the following sentences:.

- **a** I am always surprised by the (effect/affect) that horror movies have on me.
- **b** It is terrifying when you (loose/lose/loss) your friends at a very crowded concert.
- **c** Billy was far better at playing guitar (then/than) Ali was.
- **d** I was hoping that the accident didn't (effect/affect) anyone I know.
- **e** She waltzed through the door (then/than) looked right at me.
- **f** It was a sudden and surprising (loss/lose/loose) which made it hard to endure.

You be the teacher

Below is a **body paragraph** for a news report written by a Year 8 student. There are some errors in the structure of the paragraph and the spelling of some of the **commonly confused words**. Improve the structure and rewrite the paragraph with the **correct spelling of all words**.

The robbery took place at approximately 3 am. The crime was discovered when the bank manager arrived for work, noticed the front glass doors where open slightly and saw a lot of broken glass inside the entryway. Its believed their where no witnesses to the robbery. A police spokesperson said the robbers left behind DNA evidence which was being used to further they're investigation. Bank robbers have broken into a bank in North Riverdale, police say.

Now you write

It is now time for you to complete your own **news report** about a bank robbery.

1 Before you write, take some time to look at the student writing samples on the following pages as a guide to writing standards. Note the mistakes made in the Intermediate sample and try to avoid making these mistakes yourself.

2 Once you have read the two student writing samples, take some time to think about what you believe are the most important features of a news report that you need to master. Use the lines below to jot down your answer to this question:

What do you find most difficult when writing this kind of text?

3 Now look at the informative text marking criteria on page viii to double-check that you understand the requirements for a really good piece of informative writing.

Remember that you have already done your planning and drafted your headline, introduction and conclusion. Use the lines below or your own paper. Good luck!

Looking at other students' writing

News reports:
Write a report about a student riot.

Introduction
The student has included a headline and byline. The headline is succinct and engaging.

Informative techniques
The student uses clear and precise language. Third-person narrative is used to create an objective, factual tone.

Text structure
The student uses the correct structure for a news report, including an introductory paragraph, body and a conclusion.

Paragraphing
Each paragraph focuses on one point about the news story. Evidence is included in each, such as direct or indirect quotations.

Cohesion
The events reported are sequenced from the most important information to the least important information.

ADVANCED SAMPLE

STUDENTS RUN RIOT OVER 'BORING' CAFETERIA MENU

By Gordon Bennett

Police were called to a private school in Tahoma on Tuesday afternoon following reports of a riot in the cafeteria. The incident, in which several thousands of dollars worth of property damage is alleged to have occurred, was apparently a protest against what students have dubbed a 'boring' menu.

'It was the most frightening thing I've experienced in all my time as an educator,' said Ms J Melko, an arts teacher at St Sebastian College, the prestigious school at which the riot took place. 'It was crazy,' said Richard Richardson, a Year 10 student at the school. 'Everything seemed to be normal until all of a sudden food was being thrown around the room,' Richard said.

The incident is believed to have been sparked by a senior student, who cannot be named for legal reasons. Witnesses claim he threw his food to the ground before violently overturning his table, as well as trays belonging to several of his peers. Betsy Whalen, a Year 8 student at the school said, 'He got up and shouted, "If I have to eat this boring pasta one more time, I'm going to go crazy!" and then he just started throwing stuff. It was really scary,' Betsy said.

In an interview, Deputy Principal Mr. Agamenoni said that several students have been suspended, and may face expulsion following further investigation. 'I have no idea what could have led to this incident,' Mr Agamenoni said. 'The main culprits have been identified and suspended and some may face expulsion,' said Mr. Agamenoni.

Given the young age of the offenders no prosecutions were made. However Mr. Agamenoni stated that the students who were responsible for property damage would be forced to pay the cost of repairs.

Vocabulary
The language used is appropriate. Vocabulary is not too complex so it is accessible to all readers.

Sentence structure
The student uses a variety of simple, compound sentences and complex sentences, where appropriate, using mostly short, factual sentences.

Ideas
The student uses strong ideas that are relevant to the story being reported on.

Punctuation
Complex punctuation is used correctly.

Spelling
All words are spelt correctly, including more difficult words.

News reports:
Write a report about a student riot.

Introduction
The student has included a headline and byline. The headline is too wordy and needs to be more engaging. There is not enough detail about time and place.

Sentence structure
The student uses a variety of simple and compound sentences but needs to include complex sentences to explain more complex ideas.

INTERMEDIATE SAMPLE

STUDENTS RUN RIOT OVER 'BORING' CAFETERIA MENU. A RIOT OVER LUNCH TAKES PLACE IN A HIGH SCHOOL.

By gordon Bennett

Police were called to a school on Tuesday afternoon following reports of a riot. It was claimed to be a protest against a 'boring' menu.

Ms J Melko, an arts teacher at the school, said the riot was scary. 'It was crazy!!!!' said richard richardson. Someone said that everything seemed to be normal until all of a sudden food trays were being thrown around.

A senior student started the riot. Betsy Whalen, a Year 8 student at the school said the senior went wild and started throughing things around and screaming. Students were very scared.

I interviewed Mr. Agamenoni, the very hairy deputy principal, and he told me that several students have been suspended, and may be expelled. I have no idea what could have lead to this incident' Mr Agamenoni said. The once beautiful cafeteria is now broken and dirty.

Given the young age of the offenders no prosecutions were made, which is disappointing as they are very bad people. However Mr. Agamenoni stated that the students who were responsible for property damage would be forced to pay the cost of repairs.

Ideas
The student uses ideas that are relevant to the topic. Their ideas need more detail and supporting evidence in the form of direct or indirect quotations.

Paragraphing
Each paragraph features one point about the news story. The student needs to include more specific detail as well as direct quotes from witnesses to support the reporting of the incident.

Punctuation
The student uses most simple punctuation correctly but there is some missing punctuation (e.g. missing capital letters).

Informative techniques
The student uses mostly objective, non-biased language but needs to avoid personal opinion and descriptive language (e.g. *a hairy deputy principal* and *he told me*).

Spelling
Most words are spelt correctly but there are occasional spelling errors, especially in commonly confused words (e.g. 'lead' for *led* and 'throughing' for *throwing*).

Cohesion
The events reported are sequenced from the most important information to the least important information.

Text structure
The student uses the correct structure for a news report, including an introductory paragraph, body and a conclusion.

Vocabulary
The language used is mostly appropriate but more complex vocabulary is needed (e.g. *overturning* instead of *throwing*).

Note: words shaded in blue are errors.

UNIT NINE

Imaginative texts
Descriptions

Understanding the question

Descriptions:
Write a description of a haunted house.

Type of question

This question is asking you to write a particular type of imaginative text—a **description**.

The purpose of a description is to give the reader a vivid image of an object, place, person or event. A description is a **picture in words**. A description will focus on a few main elements of an object, place, person or event being described.

You are being asked to write a description of a thing—a haunted house.

Features of a description

- Aims to create a descriptive picture of an object, place, person or event
- Can occur anywhere in an imaginative text, but usually found at the beginning or in the middle
- Can create mood or atmosphere in an imaginative text
- Can use figurative language to create vivid imagery—both aural and visual
- Can be written in the first person (using the pronouns *I*, *we* or *us*) or in the third person (using the pronouns *he*, *she* or *they*, or characters' names)

The question above includes two key **content words** that tell you what you must focus on in your description—haunted house.

Look back at **Unit 1** on page 1 to find out about **content words**.

1 Use a dictionary to define the word *haunted*.

____

2 What are some synonyms for the word *house*?

____

The question above includes one **task word** that tells you what you need to do in your piece of writing.

Look back at **Unit 2** on page 13 to find out about **task words**.

3 Use a dictionary to define the word *compose*.

____

Planning and organisation

When planning a description, spend some time looking at images of the event, location, object or person you are trying to describe.

The planning stage for a description is all about **creative thinking** and using your **imagination**. At this stage it is important to **brainstorm** which of the five **senses** will be evoked in your description. The five senses are taste, touch, smell, sight and sound.

Activity 1

Look at the image of the haunted house and answer the questions. Writing in dot points is fine.

a What do you see?

____

____

b What do you hear?

____

c What do you smell?

____

d What do you taste?

____

e What do you feel?

____

Activity 2

Complete the table below by thinking of abstract nouns, action verbs, adjectives and adverbs that will **enhance** your **description**. The first one has been done for you.

Abstract nouns	Action verbs	Adjectives	Adverbs
anxiety	scurry	sinister	hurriedly

Now that you have brainstormed the senses that will be evoked in your description, it is time to **organise** the **order** in which you will present these to your reader.

Activity 3

Write the numbers 1 to 5 beside the **senses** below to reflect the order in which you will evoke them in your description. Beside each sense briefly list two or three special features of the haunted house that you wish your reader to see, hear, taste, touch and smell.

a ________ sight ______________________________

b ________ sound ______________________________

c ________ taste ______________________________

d ________ touch ______________________________

e ________ smell ______________________________

Descriptions can be written in the first person (using the pronouns *I/we/us*) or in the third person (using the pronouns *he/she/they* or characters' names). Sometimes descriptions are written with no reference to a character at all.

The first person

Often we use the **first person** in a description because we are interested in the **thoughts and experiences of one person**—the speaker. This perspective allows you to describe the emotions and thoughts the character has about other characters, events and places. This can make for a very engaging description.

For example: The rushing of the wind through the trees made me think of ghosts and I began to feel frightened.

Unfortunately the problem with the first person is that it limits the perspective the reader has of people, events and places because we can't get the feelings or thoughts of other characters.

The third person

The **third person** is very popular in novels because it allows the writer to tell the reader **things the main characters do not know about**—such as the monster lurking in the shadows behind him or her! If you want to write a description that criticises the decisions or actions made by the main characters, then the third person is the best choice for you.

For example: The wind rushed through the trees as Harry pulled his dark hood over his head in an attempt to hide his fear.

Activity 4

Below and on the next page are two short paragraphs—one is written in the first person and one is written in the third person. Your task is to rewrite each paragraph in the **opposite** form. Remember that this is not just as simple as changing pronouns from *he* to *I*—the first person should focus more on the emotions and thoughts of the speaker and the third person will focus more on the behaviour of the character being described.

a Read the passage below and then ask yourself these questions before you rewrite it.

- What emotions would you feel as you stare at the box?
- What emotions would you feel as you unwrap the paper?
- What emotions would you feel as you look at the black symbols?

b Now try to rewrite the passage below in the first person, adding in the emotions you identified above.

The box looked normal. Jenna stared at it for just a moment before she began unwrapping its crackly brown paper and loosely tied string. Underneath its boring surface was something far more interesting—a shiny red container emblazoned with foreign-looking symbols. Poking her nose close to the jagged black symbols, Jenna's eyes began to widen.

c Read the passage on the next page and then ask yourself these questions before you rewrite it.

- What is a good adjective to describe the action of someone looking up at the sky at something unusual?
- Will the reader have access to the character's past experience of watching a documentary?
- How might you describe the character's face or body to show that he or she is nervous?

d Now have a go at rewriting the passage on the next page in the third person, adding in or removing the details you identified above.

I looked up just in time to see the small black shapes begin to cloud the sky. These were like nothing I had ever seen before. Clearly they were some form of craft as they hovered together in a large, dark semicircle. I had seen something similar once in a documentary on alien aircraft and it made me nervous. As I continued to look up I felt sweat trickle down my neck and my palms began to get moist. Was this an alien invasion?

Activity 6

It is time for you to decide whether your description of the haunted house will be in the first person or the third person.

Structure

Now you've done your planning, it's time to look at the structure and key language features of a **description**.

Descriptions help readers better imagine and understand a story but sometimes they are written to capture an image of a person, place, object or event that isn't part of a story—you may, for example, want to write a description of your grandmother to help you remember her. Descriptions don't have the strict **structure** of a narrative. However, they often have **separate paragraphs** for each element of the person, place, object or event being described, as follows: **introductory** paragraph, **body** paragraphs and **concluding** paragraph.

Introductory paragraph

This paragraph lets your reader know what is being described. Typically it **sets the mood** for the rest of the description and if the description is in the first person it will indicate the character's **feelings** towards the thing or person being described.

Activity 1

Read the paragraph below. It is an example of an opening paragraph of a description.

Her name is Maria and I see her every day. Sometimes we make eye-contact and smile and sometimes there's no communication at all. Maria lives on the same street at me; I think she's lived there longer than me. When I first saw her I used to feel frightened of her crinkly old hands and gap-toothed smile. I used to hold my breath and run past her as she sat on the corner of our street. I was afraid she was a witch.

Now compose the **introductory paragraph** for a description of a person using the information below.

Age: 55
Height: average
Occupation: retired car mechanic
Hobbies: making tin soldiers
Appearance: untidy hair, slightly overweight, always wears overalls

Activity 2

It's time for you to draft the **introductory paragraph** of your description. Be sure to include what or who is being described and where the person/object/event is when being described.

Body paragraphs

The **body** of a description is a series of paragraphs that further develops the description of the thing being described. For this type of description it is best to focus on **two or three important elements** only. You might write one paragraph per distinctive feature of the thing being described. For example, if you are describing a person you may choose to write a paragraph on each of these features: appearance, voice and personality.

Activity 3

Rearrange the following sentences to make a sensible piece of **descriptive writing** about the front yard of a haunted house.

- **a** The lawn is overgrown and shows no signs of having been cared for in years.
- **b** The verandah of the house hangs dangerously on one side and the steps lead nowhere.
- **c** A cat scurries underneath the rusty Kombi camper sagging in the driveway.
- **d** This is the yard of no return.
- **e** Accidentally throwing a ball into this yard would be tragic. There would be no returning.
- **f** Behind the van leers the house.

Activity 4

Return to the planning you did earlier in this unit. Use this information to draft one of your **body paragraphs**.

Concluding paragraph

The final paragraph of your description is **a final, lasting picture of the thing being described**—the person, object, event or scene. Remind your reader of the main features of whatever has been described and end with a final, memorable statement about it. Below is an example **concluding paragraph** (about Maria from Activity 1) for you to use as a guide.

It's strange how swiftly our picture of someone can change. When I used to focus only on Maria's old-fashioned clothes, her shabby bags of odds and ends and the dirty corner where she spent her days, I never allowed myself to see her as a person. It's taken me some time and courage, but now I know that even though Maria doesn't have a house, she is part of our community.

Activity 5

Return to the planning you did earlier in this unit. Use this information to draft the **concluding paragraph** of your description.

____

____

____

____

Language feature

Figurative language

News reports are written to provide information about current events. The purpose is simply to Descriptions are imaginative and engaging pieces of writing. Descriptions aim to **engage readers by creating pictures through words**. The best descriptions encourage the reader to use his or her imagination to picture a person, object, event or location. A useful technique to enliven the imagination of readers is figurative language.

Figurative language is the use of figures of speech to **describe** something by **comparing** it to something else. Figurative language forces a reader to use their imagination. Three common **figures of speech** that are used in descriptions are **metaphor**, **simile** and **personification**.

Metaphor

A **metaphor** is a **direct comparison** of one thing to another.

For example: *Lucy is a pig* directly compares Lucy to a pig.

This technique engages the imagination of the reader as he or she is forced to imagine Lucy as looking like or behaving like a pig.

Here are some more examples of metaphors.

- I am a star.
- Australia is a melting-pot.
- The library is a gateway to another world.
- All the world is a stage.

Activity 1

Write **metaphors** to describe these events and people.

a a messy child ______________________

b a moody teenager ______________________

c a bossy teacher ______________________

d a businessman ______________________

e a football game ______________________

f a rock concert ______________________

g a car crash ______________________

h a school playground ______________________

Simile

A **simile** is a figure of speech that **compares two unlike things**, often using the words *like* or *as*. This is a less direct comparison than a metaphor.

For example: Lucy eats like a pig.

A simile helps the reader to **imagine** the person, situation, event or object being described by comparing it to something else.

For example: Her smiled warmed the room like the sun.

When similies are overused they become clichés. It is best to make up your own original similes as these will be more effective in encouraging your reader to use his or her imagination.

Activity 2

For each of the clichéd **similes** below, write a more interesting comparison using *like* or *as*.

a as bright as a button ______________________

b like two peas in a pod ______________________

c as dead as a doornail ______________________

d as quick as lightning ______________________

e as blind as a bat ______________________

Personification

Personification is when you **give human qualities to non-human things**. The purpose of this figure of speech is to **encourage your readers to imagine** an object in new ways.

For example: The tree branch grabbed at her legs.

In this example the tree is given the human ability to *grab* at something and it encourages the reader to imagine the tree as threatening and cruel.

Activity 3

For each **figure of speech** state whether it is a similie, metaphor or personification.

a Bianca carried the world on her shoulders. ____________________

b The car's engine snarled. ____________________

c She fell to the ground like a bag of lead. ____________________

Activity 4

Identify if the **figure of speech** is used to create a **visual** or **aural image**.

a Johnny opened the door and was hit by a wall of sound. ____________________

b A thousand stars that looked like shining diamonds lit up the sky. ____________________

c The guitar screamed and screeched. ____________________

d The football stadium was a tidal wave of emotion. ____________________

Language feature

Variety of sentence types

A wonderful way to engage your reader is to use a **variety** of different **sentence types**. Sometimes we fall into the habit of just using one particular sentence type and this can become boring for the reader.

Short sentences create **action** and **tension**. Sometimes a writer may use just one word as a sentence.

For example: It was time. Balin knew it was now or never. He thrust off his jacket and shoes. Splash! The water was freezing. He sped towards the figure in the distance.

Questions may be asked in **dialogue** or as **rhetorical questions** which show the main character thinking about his or her situation. This technique creates a **mood** of **contemplation**.

For example: I dart through the doorway and just miss being hit by the swinging door as it slams shut. What am I doing here? Do I really believe that a girl from Parramatta can save the world?

The purpose of **exclamations** is to indicate **surprise** and create a **mood** of either **excitement** or **tension**.

For example: He lunged forward onto the second pillar. Now all he had to do was grab that final flag and he was the winner. Whoosh! He made it! Victory at last!

Activity 5

Which of the **sentence types** outlined above are used in these examples?

a Ouch. The ground was hard. He must run. ______

b Can I go on? The competitors are so aggressive. ______

c I opened the envelope carefully, my breathing heavy. I won! ______

d This can't be right, can it? Mrs. Canton said I was the winner. Me?! ______

e Could I really be the winner of the tournament? ______

f There is no way I am going sailing in that terrifying storm! It's practically a cyclone! ______

g I see him. He's right behind the pillar. I have no choice. It's him or me. ______

Spotlight *on spelling*

Adding suffixes

You have already looked at adding suffixes while working through this book. In this unit you will focus on different types of suffixes and how they change parts of speech.

Creating adjectives by adding *able* to nouns

Adjectives are used frequently in descriptions to help your readers imagine the object, place, event or person you are describing.

Nouns ending in *e* (such as *value*) drop the *e* and add *able*.

For example: value → valu**able**

Activity 1

Complete the table below.

Noun	Adjective
a accept	
b	comfortable
c	desirable
d cure	
e memory	
f	perceivable

g shake	
h	valuable
i	unspeakable

Creating adjectives by adding 'ant' and 'ious' to a noun

Another way to create an **adjective** is to add a suffix to a noun. These can be quite tricky. See the following specific rules for each.

ant

When writing nouns ending in *ance* drop the *ce* and add *t*.

For example: abundan**ce** → abundan**t**

Activity 2

For each of the nouns below, write its **adjectival** form then use it in a sentence. The first one has been done for you.

a abundance abundant

The wattle is abundant at this time of year.

b elegance ______________________

____

c irrelevance ______________________

____

d significance ______________________

____

e arrogance ______________________

____

f resistance ______________________

____

g tolerance ______________________

____

ious

Some nouns ending in *y* form adjectives ending in *ious*.

For example:
glor**y** → glor**ious**
anxiet**y** → anx**ious**
curiosit**y** → cur**ious**

You can usually hear the long *e* sound in the word and this is a help when spelling.

For example: glor-i(ee)-ous.

Note: many *ious* adjectives do not derive from a noun ending in *y*, such as *obvious*, *devious* or *religious*.

Activity 3

Complete the table below.

Noun	Adjective
hilarity	
anxiety	
glory	
luxury	
space	
variety	
infection	
fury	
deviant	
contagion	

You be the teacher

Below is a **descriptive paragraph** written by a Year 8 student. There are some errors in the use of figurative language and the spelling of some of the words with suffixes. There is also one unnecessary sentence. Rewrite the paragraph below with more appropriate **figurative language**, with the unnecessary sentence removed and with the **correct spelling of all words**.

The setting sun threw gloryous streaks of red and orange across the darkening sky and the air felt thick like a pancake. I wondered if I had the wrong address because this house looked much too big and far too old. The house loomed ahead like a giant ladybeetle and I began to feel very uncumftable. My lungs refused to take in the unfriendly air and I found myself wheezing and aching to be anywhere but here. It is the second of May. Dark windows stared into my anxous mind.

Now you write

It is now time for you to complete your own **description** of a haunted house.

1 Before you write, take some time to look at the student writing samples on the following pages as a guide to writing standards. Note the mistakes made in the Intermediate sample and try to avoid making these mistakes yourself.

2 Once you have read the two student writing samples, take some time to think about what you believe are the most important features of a description that you need to master. Use the lines below to jot down your answer to this question:

What do you find most difficult when writing this kind of text?

3 Now look at the imaginative text marking criteria on page ix to double-check that you understand the requirements for a really good piece of imaginative writing.

Remember that you have already done your planning and drafted your introduction, one body paragraph and conclusion. Use your own paper. Good luck!

Looking at other students' writing

Descriptions:

Compose a description of a remote location.

Opening
The student sets the mood of the description and clearly indicates the attitude towards the thing/person being described.

Vocabulary
Difficult vocabulary is used. A variety of adjectives and adverbs are used to enhance the images created.

ADVANCED SAMPLE

There are few hills out here. Those that can be seen are certainly not mountains—small enough for an enthusiastic child to run to the top and claim to be king of the castle.

Besides the occasional hill, this landscape is flat as far as the eye can see. The red ground is covered by shrubs that resemble fuzzy-haired children. Only the very tough animal or reptile could survive out here.

Far out there, beyond the hill, a dust devil raises itself tall and angry. Its feet are thick with desert sand that whirls and twirls. Its head is loose and uncontrolled. It looks like a quick-footed woman with long red hair who dances in circles. But the dust devil's time is limited and shortly its strength will weaken. The sand will settle back to the ground to be warmed by the bursting sun.

Ribboning through this barren land is a silver highway; it glistens and sparkles as if it were encrusted with millions of crushed diamonds. Brave travellers scurry along this road in the safety of their cars.

Under the broken dome of blue sky, this land remains untouched. This is Australia.

Narrative techniques
The student uses descriptive language to engage the reader's imagination. Poetic devices enhance the description.

Text structure
The description is well structured so that new aspects of the landscape are revealed slowly to create interest.

Paragraphing
A new paragraph is used to introduce a new aspect of the landscape.

Sentence structure
A variety of sentence lengths are used to avoid monotony and create interest.

Ideas
The theme of the description (a remote landscape) is sustained throughout.

Punctuation
Correct punctuation is used. Complex punctuation is used where required.

Cohesion
There is continuity of ideas throughout the description—focus is always on the landscape.

Spelling
All words are spelt correctly. There is frequent inclusion of difficult or challenging words.

Descriptions:
Compose a description of a remote location.

Opening
The student attempts to set the mood of the description but there is no real indication of the attitude towards the thing/person being described. There is no clear indication of scene.

Sentence structure
The student attempts to use a variety of sentence lengths but there are too many simple sentences (e.g. *There is a road that runs through the land.*).

INTERMEDIATE SAMPLE

It's really flat there. There is only one hill and it is medium sized, probably the size a kid could run up without even geting too tired. From the top of the medium-sized hill would be a very good view of the really flat land out there.

The ground is very dry and is red like a berry. There are some little small bushes that are not too big. Maybe there are some little grey lizards living under the small green bushes. It would be hard and difficult to live in a place as dry and hot and flat as this place.

There are dust devils out here. Dust devils are big and large spirals of brown and red dust that spins in the air and looks like a hurricane but only smaller. The dust devil spins around very past and dust goes everywhere. it looks a bit like someone running around over the hot dry ground. it doesn't last very long and then it is gone.

There is a road that runs through the land. It is a long, silver, glitering road that looks a bit like it has glass in it because it shines in the sun. The people who drive on this road drive fast because they don't want to be stuck in this desert with its really strong heat and nothing to do. The cars drive really fast?

It is a special land out here because it hasn't got many houses on it and it is a bit like a secret. This is Australia.

Narrative techniques
There is some use of descriptive language to engage the reader's imagination. Simplistic poetic devices enhance the description (e.g. the simile *red like a berry*).

Paragraphing
A new paragraph is used to introduce a new aspect of the landscape.

Cohesion
There is continuity of ideas throughout the description. The student uses somewhat repetitive sentence beginnings (e.g. *There*).

Vocabulary
The student attempts to use a variety of adjectives and adverbs but needs to use more interesting words (e.g. *little* could be *miniscule*; *good view* could be *unobstructed view*).

Ideas
The student touches on the theme of the description (a remote landscape) throughout.

Text structure
The student uses the correct structure of a description but the writing lacks detail.

Spelling
Most words are spelt correctly but some words with suffixes are spelt incorrectly (e.g. 'geting' instead of *getting*).

Punctuation
The student mostly uses correct punctuation but there are some errors (e.g. capital letters and misuse of question mark).

Note: words shaded in blue are errors.

UNIT TEN

10 Imaginative texts
Short stories

Understanding the question

Short stories:
Write a short story based on the title 'The Crash'.

Type of question

This question is asking you to write a type of imaginative text—a **short story**.

The purpose of a short story is to **entertain the reader** and **engage** his or her **emotions**, **imagination** and **thoughts**. Short stories are brief and as such they tend to focus on one character, setting and event. You are being asked to write a short story about an event—a crash.

Features of a short story

- Aims to entertain the reader and engage his or her emotions, imagination and thoughts
- Develops characters through dialogue, descriptions of actions and distinctive voices
- Action occurs in a distinctive setting
- Structure: orientation, complication, resolution
- Uses a variety of sentence structures: simple, compound, complex
- Has strong action verbs and emotive language
- Uses figurative language
- Uses first-person or third-person narrative

This question asks you to write a short story and gives you a title for the story. There are three **content words** in this question.

title based the crash

1 Why do writers give their **short stories** titles?

____

____

____

____

2 Use a dictionary to define the word *crash*.

____

____

____

3 Use the internet or a thesaurus to find synonyms for the word *crash*.

Planning and organisation

TIP Great stories require **careful planning**. Before you begin writing it is a good idea to spend some time thinking about the **plot** of your short story.

You must **plan** before every piece of writing you do. When planning for your short story you will:

- decide on the **main setting** and **character** for your story
- plot the action of your story using a **plot graph**.

Activity 1

Your story will be titled 'The Crash'. List some different types of crashes that could feature in your story. Remember that the crash does not need to be on the road or between vehicles. It could be a comet crashing to Earth, a stock-market crash or an emotional 'crash' from holding in a secret for too long.

Activity 2

From the options above, select the type of crash that will feature in your short story.

Activity 3

Now that you have established the type of crash that will feature in your short story, you need to do some thinking and research to help develop the setting, characters and plot. Use your own experience or research information to fill in the following table.

See	Hear	Smell	Taste	Feel

Activity 4

In a short story you really only have enough space to fully develop one or two main characters. Who will be the character(s) in your short story? Fill in the table below.

Character trait	My character
gender	
age	
occupation	
marital status	
personality	
nationality	
physical appearance	

Activity 5

You now need to think about where your story will take place. Your story can take place anywhere: on a bus, in the jungle, on the moon, under the sea or in a classroom.

Identify two **settings** that could feature in your story. For each setting write one sentence explaining why you have chosen that setting.

Setting one:

____

____

____

Setting two:

____

____

____

Structure

Short stories are an imaginative form of writing and many writers don't stick to a strict structure. However, it's a good idea to master the traditional narrative structure before you move on to a more tricky experimental style. The following outline is the **traditional narrative structure** and has been used for thousands of years. You will be able to plot most of your favourite films using this structure!

The traditional **narrative structure** has three main parts: **orientation**, **complication** and **resolution**. This structure helps you **develop your character** and **create action** to engage your readers.

Orientation

The **orientation** is typically no longer than one or two paragraphs. In this section you **introduce your setting** and your **character**. A strong orientation will **grab the reader's attention** and make them want to keep reading. Creating action or intrigue can do this.

Activity 1

Look at the two short opening paragraphs below and answer the questions below them.

Glass fell from the windscreen and shattered onto the bonnet. Smoke, grey and greasy, poured from the engine. The first impact had knocked Aziz out momentarily but this second impact brought him back to the surface of reality. Through his badly swollen eyes he saw petrol dripping onto the road and the flickering flames.

a Does this opening use **action** or **intrigue** to hook the reader? ______________________

b Where is this story set? ______________________

c Who is the main character? ______________________

Kalini trod carefully on the Martian soil, hoping her gentle steps wouldn't wake a thing. The air was thick and it made breathing without a mask difficult. Determined to make it back to base, Kalini refused to look back at her badly damage vehicle.

d Does this opening use **action** or **intrigue** to hook the reader? ______________________

e Where is this story set? ______________________

f Who is the main character? ______________________

Activity 2

Now it's your turn to write the **orientation** to your story titled 'The Crash'.

Complication

The **complication** is a series of paragraphs that **develops the main action** of a story. It involves the introduction of a problem that the main character must overcome. This leads to a scene of **increased tension** where the character is faced with some kind of danger or important decision.

Return to your earlier planning where you graphed the plot of your short story. Use this information to complete the next activity.

Activity 3

a What problem must your character overcome? (e.g. road rage or being stranded on the moon)

-
-
-

b What dangerous situation or difficult decision will your character face? (e.g. confronting an angry driver or a solo spacewalk to the next spaceship)

-
-
-

c Write two or three dot points to describe what will occur at each stage of your short story.

-
-
-

Resolution

The **resolution** follows the **climax** in a short story. This is where the problem is overcome and life begins to return to normal. Many stories include a final scene called a *coda* where the character reflects on his or her experience and the lesson learned.

Write some notes about the **resolution** to your story titled 'The Crash'. This may take the form of a draft or a few dot-points.

Language feature

Descriptive langauge

Descriptive language helps a reader **visualise** the settings, characters and events of a short story. Often writers will use a variety of techniques to help **enliven** the reader's senses: sight, smell, taste, touch and sound.

One problem that new writers suffer from is the overuse of adjectives. Often when we want to describe a person, place, event or thing we use adjectives. It is okay to use adjectives sometimes, but if they are used too often, or if too many are used, they can lose their impact on the reader.

Here is an example of an 'over-written' sentence:

The large, dark car roared quickly like a cheetah down the long, empty street.

This sentence would be much better if it eliminated some adjectives and the adverb. See?

The dark car roared down the empty street.

Following are two strategies for creating descriptive language without overusing adjectives.

Sometimes we get carried away with the way we are writing and forget that we are writing a story to be read by someone else. While figurative language can be effective in small doses, it isn't necessary to describe every detail. Often a **strong action verb** tells your reader more about a character than three sentences of description.

For example: The sentence *She was worried that she would be late so she* ***ran*** *like the wind to the shops* can be more effectively expressed as *She* ***rushed*** *to the shops.*

Activity 1

For each common verb, write a **strong action verb** that could be used instead. The first one has been done for you.

a run ______gallop______

b walk ____________

c talk ____________

d smile ____________

e touch ____________

f throw ____________

g cry ____________

h laugh ____________

i yell ____________

j jump ____________

Concrete detail

We all know that it is important to create **believable people**, **objects**, **events** and **places** in short stories. Sometimes new writers include too much general detail and not enough **concrete detail**. To engage with your reader's imagination, try adding some concrete detail; so instead of saying *a* **car** *was parked in the driveway* say *a* **'74 Kombi camper** *was parked in the driveway*.

Activity 2

For each of the general detail, give a **specific concrete example**. The first one has been done for you.

a drink ______Fanta______

b television show ____________

c suburb ____________

d shoes ____________

e car ____________

f house ____________

g film ____________

h book ____________

i t-shirt ____________

j mobile phone ____________

Activity 3

Below are five very general sentences. Rewrite them to give more **concrete detail** about the underlined central noun. The first one has been done for you.

1. The cat stared out the window. The relaxed Persian cat stared out of the window.
2. I grabbed a can of drink. ____________________
3. Jessica really enjoyed the game. ____________________
4. The dinner was delicious. ____________________
5. Jonno is addicted to playing a video game. ____________________

Spotlight *on spelling*

Tense

Short stories can be written in the past tense or the present tense. Young writers often get confused with tense and forget to ensure that they are using the correct tense form of the verbs. This section will look at how adding a suffix can **change the tense** of a verb. You will also learn how to add the suffix *ly* to turn an adjective into an adverb. Knowing the rules for adding suffixes can really help you spell words correctly.

Adding the suffixes 'ing' and 'ed'

A **suffix** is added to the end of a root word and changes both the spelling and the form of the word. It is good to remember that a suffix cannot stand on its own. A suffix is always spelt fully.

Most past-tense and present-participle verb forms are simply made by adding *ed* and *ing*. However, when adding the suffix *ed* or *ing* to a **root word ending in the letter *e*** you must drop the *e* before adding the suffix.

For example: revers**e** → revers**ing**

If adding the suffix *ed* or *ing* to a root word ending in a **vowel and a single consonant**, the consonant at the end of the word must double before adding the suffix.

For example: fl**op** → fl**opping**

Note: in the above example, the vowel is *o* and is followed by the single consonant *p*.

Simple past and present

Adding the suffix *ed* to most verbs makes a verb **past tense**.

For example: look → look**ed**

Adding the suffix *ing* to most verbs makes a **present participle**.

For example: crash → crash**ing**

Activity 1

Add the suffix *ed* and *ing* to the root words in the table to create the **present participle** and **past tense** form of the words. The first one has been done for you.

Root word	Present tense	Past tense
bath	bathing	bathed
purchase		
dance		
rebel		
extend		
hope		
reverse		
mix		
resign		
examine		
exercise		
confront		
prop		
admit		
permit		

Adverbs

Adverbs describe an action. Adverbs are used often in imaginative writing because they help the reader **imagine** how an action is performed.

Adding the suffix *ly* to most adjectives creates an adverb.

For example: quick → quick**ly**

When adding the suffix *ly* to an adjective that ends in *l* you end up with a double *l* in the word.

For example: grateful → gratefu**lly**

When adding the suffix *ly* to an adjective that ends in *y*, you drop the *y* and add *i* before adding *ly*.

For example: happy → happ**ily**

Activity 2

Add the **suffix** *ly* to the following adjectives to create **adverbs**.

a hasty ____________________

b swift ____________________

c sure ______________________

d horizontal ______________________

e stealthy ______________________

f successful ______________________

g third ______________________

h public ______________________

i critical ______________________

j unconscious ______________________

k hopeful ______________________

l aggressive ______________________

m sunny ______________________

n awkward ______________________

o ideal ______________________

p breezy ______________________

q technical ______________________

r original ______________________

s subtle ______________________

t undeniable ______________________

u true ______________________

v decisive ______________________

You be the teacher

Here is the **complication section** of a short story written by a Year 8 student. There are some errors in the structure of the paragraph and the spelling of some of the words with **suffixes**. Improve the **structure** and rewrite the paragraph with the **correct spelling of all words**.

The fire extinguisher! A strong smell of petrol slowely filled the air and Jai felt his head spin.

Looking desprity to his left his eye caught sight of a bright red cylinder. It was stuck. Getting out of the car imediatly was all Jai had been able to think of and now he found himself trapped. It was his only hope, but could he reach it? Pushing on the orange button, Jai tried once again to release himself from the seatbelt.

Now you write

It is now time for you to complete your own **short story** titled 'The Crash'.

1 Before you write, take some time to look at the student writing samples on the following pages as a guide to writing standards. Note the mistakes made in the Intermediate sample and try to avoid making these mistakes yourself.

2 Once you have read the two student writing samples, take some time to think about what you believe are the most important features of a short story that you need to master. Use the lines below to jot down your answer to this question:

What do you find most difficult when writing this kind of text?

3 Now look at the imaginative text marking criteria on page ix to double-check that you understand the requirements for a really good piece of imaginative writing.

Remember that you have already done your planning and drafted your orientation, complication and resolution. Use your own paper. Good luck!

Looking at other students' writing

Short stories:

Write a short story with the title 'The first day'.

Orientation
There is a strong orientation that grabs the reader's attention through the use of intrigue.

Narrative techniques
The descriptive language engages the reader's imagination. Humour and emotive language are used well.

Text structure
The short story is well structured, featuring obvious orientation, complication and resolution.

Paragraphing
A new paragraph is used to introduce a main part of the story's action. Tension is built effectively.

Cohesion
There is continuity of ideas throughout the description—the focus is always on James's first day.

ADVANCED SAMPLE

THE FIRST DAY

James Donnelly: *First day. Feeling sick in the stomach.*

He knew his mum would see his Facebook status and start fussing about how first days are always daunting. But he didn't regret posting it. Maybe he might get a comment from Max, Johnno or—less likely—Jess. Surely they would agree with him; first days are the pits. Max might even post a YouTube clip of a kid being chased by a goat or something. Just to cheer him up.

For as long as he could remember, James's mum had tortured him by singing along to the cheesy tunes on the car radio. It's not that she has a bad voice, it's just that she sings loudly with the car windows down. This morning James's mother was treating the passing neighbourhood to her rendition of Meatloaf's 'I would do anything for love'. James just hoped she would give her larynx a rest before they got to their destination.

A looming black fence topped with angry spikes was James's only memory of his new school. Thinking of it now he began to regret sitting the selective high school test. He had aced it and was quickly accepted into the nearest selective school, Greenwell Selective Campus. He remembered vividly the reaction of Max, Johnno and Jess when he broke the news that he wouldn't be going with them to Dalyson Comprehensive. The handball gang was being disbanded, all because of his IQ. He still felt awful. Jess had barely spoken to him since he told her. On their last day of Year 6 she had given him a quick hug and pressed a small piece of paper into his hand. It simply said, 'Get 'em geek. Love Jess.' yet it had burned a hole into his heart.

Having hastily escaped from his mother's music-box on wheels, James found himself in a sea washing towards the mouth of the black fence. He swallowed hard and let himself be caught up in the tide. Inside, the school itself looked normal and unthreatening. He surveyed his surrounds and noted the usual crowds: the pretty girls with perfect hair and straight teeth; the surfer boys all blonde hair and brown skin; and way down the back he could see the handball kids. These were his kind and seeing them brought a smile to his lips.

***

With five minutes of sneaky internet time on his mum's old PC, James logged in to Facebook to share his reflections on his first day of high school.

Vocabulary
Complex vocabulary is used. A variety of adjectives and strong verbs are used to enhance the images created (e.g. *tortured* and *fussing*).

Sentence structure
A variety of sentence lengths are used to avoid monotony and create interest. Short sentences create drama.

Ideas
The theme of the short story (a first day) is developed and sustained throughout.

Punctuation
Correct punctuation is used. Complex punctuation is used where required.

Spelling
All words are spelt correctly. There is frequent inclusion of difficult or challenging words (e.g. *looming*, *advantage* and *embarrassed*).

Short stories:
Write a short story with the title 'The first day'.

Narrative techniques
There is some use of descriptive language to engage the reader's imagination. The student uses a simplistic attempt at humour and there is no use of poetic devices.

Sentence structure
The student attempts to use a variety of sentence lengths, but there are too many simple sentences (e.g. 'He was feeling a bit sad.').

Opening
The opening attempts to grab the reader's attention through the use of intrigue. The writing lacks emotion.

Ideas
The writer touches on the theme of the description (a first day) throughout, but the ideas are underdeveloped.

INTERMEDIATE SAMPLE

THE FIRST DAY

James Donnelly: *First day. Feeling sick in the stomach.*

He knew his mum would see his Facebook status and get worried but he didn't care. his friends might agree with him and that would make him feel a lot better. he was feeling a bit sad.

On the way to school James's mum kept singing in the car and it was so embarasing. She always sang with the windows of the car down and people would stare at them both like they were freaks. He wished that her voice would stop working one day so he wouldn't be so embarrassed by her!!! He didn't want her to be singing when they made it to the place they were going.

The fence around the school was the only thing that James could remember. It looked big and scary and he started wishing that he hadn't applied to come to a selective high school. He is a really smart and it was easy for him to get in to the selective class. His friends from his old school were really upset with him and this made him feel bad. The girl he liked told him he would do well at the new school but he just felt sad because he couldn't be with her.

James got out of his mum's car and waved goodbye. There were so many students that James felt freaked by them. He was getting annoied because there were a lot of students pushing. The school was OK when he got inside and that made him feel a bit better. He noticed that there were the same types of students in this school as there were in his last school. It wasn't too long and he found some handball kids, these were people he felt cumftable with.

***

When he got home he used his mum's PC and typed up a message on Facebook:

James Donnelly: *Handball is awesome at Greenwell Selective.*

Paragraphing
A new paragraph is used to introduce a new idea about the first day.

Punctuation
Correct punctuation is mostly used. There are some errors (e.g. capital letters and misuse of exclamation marks).

Cohesion
There is continuity of ideas throughout the short story but the student uses repetitive sentence beginnings, (e.g. 'He did' and 'His friends').

Text structure
The student uses the correct structure of a short story but it lacks detail.

Vocabulary
The student attempts to use a variety of adjectives and strong verbs but needs to use more interesting words (e.g. 'big' could be 'gigantic'; 'really upset' could be 'devastated').

Spelling
Most words are spelt correctly. Some words with suffixes are spelt incorrectly (e.g. 'annoied' instead of *annoyed* and 'embarasing' instead of *embarrassing*).

Note: words shaded in blue are errors.

UNIT ELEVEN

Imaginative texts
Biographies

Understanding the question

Biographies:

Write a biography of your best friend.

Type of question

This question is asking you to write a particular type of imaginative text—a **biography**.

This question is very direct, using the **task words** *write a biography* to tell you exactly what you need to do.

Sometimes when you're required to write a biography the question might ask you to *write/tell the life story* of someone.

Features of a biography

- Aims to recount a series of facts about a person's life in chronological order
- Opening paragraph provides important information such as name, date of birth and what the person is best known for
- Body paragraphs recount different events in the person's life (are generally chronological in sequence)
- Concluding paragraph usually makes an overall comment on the person's life
- Uses formal and mostly objective language
- Is written in the past tense
- Uses time connectives to indicate the sequence of events

1 Use a dictionary to define the word ***biography***.

____

____

2 Write down a list of at least five people you know whose life story you might like to write about. Circle the name of the person you have chosen to write about.

a ______________________________

b ______________________________

c ______________________________

d ______________________________

e ______________________________

Planning and organisation

TIP Even though you might know a lot about your topic—it's still really important to **plan**! Take some time to research and organise your ideas carefully.

Activity 1

Use the following spider-map to brainstorm what you already know about your best friend.

Activity 2

Now it's time to do some **research**. Research is helpful even if you know your subject very well!

1 Use the questions below to interview the subject of your biography. Record your notes from the conversation in the table below.

TIP When writing a biography on someone you don't know, you will need to use books or the internet to help you answer these questions. Always make sure your source is reliable by checking the date of publication and that the writer is credible!

What is your full name?	
When and where were you born?	
Where did you grow up and what was it like there?	
What did you most enjoy doing as a child?	

Where did you go to school? What is your strongest memory of being there?	
Tell me about a memorable moment in your life, a time you will never forget.	
What is your greatest achievement to date?	
What are the goals you are still working towards?	
When people look back at your life, how do you want to be remembered?	

Structure

A **biography** tells about events that have happened to people during their lives. Its **structure** is usually a **record of events** in the order they happened and contains the following: an **introductory** paragraph, **body** paragraphs and **concluding** paragraph. Biographies are typically written in the third person using the pronouns *he* or *she*. Sometimes a biography is personal and is written in the first person using the pronouns *me* or *I*. If so, it is called an **autobiography**. Biographies are always written in the **past tense**.

Introductory paragraph

The **first paragraph** of a biography is important as it must provide the reader with a brief **overview** of the person the biography is about. It hints at what the person is best known for. The introduction features proper nouns such as the names of places and people—this helps **orient** the reader.

For example: Martin Luther King was the leader of the American Civil Rights Movement that took place in the 1950s and 1960s. He fought against racism and pledged to make the world a better place.

Activity 1

Below are sentences for a student's **introductory paragraph** for a biography of Australian poet, Oodgeroo Noonuccal. Unfortunately the sentences are out of order. Re-order these sentences from 1 to 4 to make the introduction paragraph correct.

a ________ She worked tirelessly as a poet and activist for Indigenous rights.

b ________ Oodgeroo Noonuccal was born Kathleen Jean Mary Ruska, on Minjerribah (the Stradbroke Islands).

c ________ She was the first Aboriginal Australian to publish a book of poetry.

d ________ In 1970, she was appointed a Member of the Order of the British Empire (Civil) for services to the community.

Activity 2

Use the information below to write an introduction to a biography on Michael Jackson.

Born: 29 August 1958

Died: 25 June 2009

Occupation: pop singer

Claim to fame: 'King of Pop' and most successful entertainer of all time

Death: died tragically from a heart attack at the age of 50

Activity 3

It is now time for you to draft your **introduction** to the biography of your best friend.

Body paragraphs

Biographies recall events in the order in which they happened. The **body** of a biography is a series of **chronological paragraphs** detailing important events in your subject's life. You need a new paragraph when there is a change in time or place or a new event is introduced.

Cohesion

Cohesion is important in body paragraphs to help the reader follow the sequence of events and see the connection between ideas in a paragraph. Two important ways to achieve cohesion is through use of **connectives** and **pronouns**.

- Use **connectives** to indicate when events occurred.
  For example: firstly, then, next, later, finally
  (See the 'Language Features' section for more information.)
- Use **pronouns** to show the connections in a paragraph by referring to people, places, ideas and events in the biography.
  For example: he, she, it, they, this, such, there, here

The following is an example of a **body paragraph**—the pronouns are underlined and the connective is in bold.

King became well known for the passionate talks he gave in front of large crowds. His most memorable speech was at the Washington rally in 1963 when gave his famous, 'I have a dream' speech. This was an important moment in the Civil Rights Movement and King's speech rallied many more to support the anti-racism movement. **Afterwards**, this speech would be written on a plaque on the spot where King delivered the speech.

Activity 4

Here are a Year 7 student's notes for the **body paragraphs** for a biography on Michael Jackson. They are a bit jumbled. Put the events in chronological order in preparation for writing the paragraphs.

a __________ He was inducted into the Rock and Roll Music Hall of Fame in 2001.

b __________ In 1979 he became the first solo artist to have four singles from the same album in the top 10 of the *Billboard* Hot 100.

c __________ He married his long-time friend Lisa Marie Presley when he was 36.

d __________ He joined the Jackson 5 in 1964 when he was 8 years old.

Activity 5

Circle the **pronouns** and underline the **proper nouns** they are referring to in these sentences. The first one has been done for you.

a The Australian actor Heath Ledger, was best known for (his) role in 'Batman'.

b Shakespeare enjoyed making his audience laugh. He often included clowns just for this purpose.

c After winning gold at the 2000 Olympic Games, Cathy Freeman draped herself with the Aboriginal flag. This caused outrage because unofficial flags are banned from the Olympic Games.

d Keira Knightly is one of the most popular female actresses today. She has been nominated for many acting awards during her career.

Concluding paragraph

A **conclusion** is necessary as it leaves the reader with a **memorable image** or **idea** about the person's life or contribution.

For example:

Despite having died tragically well before his time, Martin Luther King continues to inspire people every day. His passionate belief in a unified, harmonious world is celebrated through the continued dedication of freedom activists in America and around the world.

Activity 6

It is now time for you to write a draft of your **concluding paragraph** to the biography of your best friend.

Language feature

Connectives

As you learned in Unit 2, connectives are linking words or phrases that show the **connections between ideas**. In a biography, **connectives** are also often used to express **when** an event happened as part of a sequence of time.

These connectives are also known as connecting adverbs. Connectives usually come first in a sentence.

Anyway	Consequently
Moreover	Nevertheless

For example: **Furthermore**, Mary felt isolated by her lack of friends at the new school.

Some connectives express time.

firstly (secondly, thirdly, etc)		finally	then	next
here	now	lastly	meanwhile	after	before
while	every time	just then	later	eventually

Note: connectives are different from conjunctions. **Conjunctions** connect clauses or phrases and usually come in the middle of a sentence.

The following are examples of conjunctions.

but	because	and	so	until

Activity 1

Underline the correct **connective** in these sentences.

a (Then/Here) he moved to Texas to study anthropology.

b (Every time/Finally) she had found her true calling in life—as a singer.

c (Just then/Eventually) Thomas would discover that football was not to be his final career.

d (Thirdly/In summary) in the major championships, Stella tragically broke her left ankle.

e (Firstly/Eventually) after the breakdown in his relationship, Jones left the country to find a new life.

f (Since then/Meanwhile), the unprecedented success of their single meant that the band could complete their first studio album.

Activity 2

Choose the correct **connective** to complete these sentences.

Meanwhile	Lastly	Since then	Until then	Next

a Jasmine was busy in the kitchen making cupcakes. ____________________ Joel was playing video games in the lounge room.

b The last time I saw Joe he was only 2 years old. ____________________ he has grown so much.

c I am going to the shops in a quarter of an hour. ____________________ I am going to sit quietly and read.

d First Shani instructed us on how to insert a file into the website.

____________________ she showed us how to embed images and video.

Activity 3

Choose two **connectives** from the box to complete the following biography body paragraph.

Lastly	Since then	Until then
Next	However	Finally

In Atlanta, Georgia, Jones was experiencing difficulty with his back. However, he had tried a variety of different medications and treatments to no avail. ____________________, in June, a breakthrough emerged. Jones's new assistant recommended he try yoga and it seemed to have a positive effect. ____________________, through his dedication to his yoga routine, his back problems diminished.

Spotlight *on spelling*

Adding suffixes to words that end in *y*

You have learnt about suffixes throughout the book. In this unit we're going to look at something a bit more tricky—adding **suffixes** to words ending in **y**.

If the final *y* in the word follows a consonant (e.g. *d, t, l, f, r*) change the *y* to an *i* when adding suffixes, except for *ing*.

For example: **fly** + *er* = fl**ier**
par**ty** + *ed* = part**ied**
app**ly** + *ing* = appl**ying**

With the *ing* suffix you always keep the final *y*.

For example: fly + *ing* = fl**ying**
party + *ing* = part**ying**

If the final *y* follows a vowel (*a, e, i, o, u*) keep the *y* when adding any suffix.

For example: empl**oy** + *ed* → emplo**yed**
empl**oy** + *ing* → emplo**ying**

Activity 1

Add the **suffix** *ed* to the verbs below.

a enjoy ______________________

b apply ______________________

c stay ______________________

d try ______________________

e play ______________________

f tidy ______________________

g delay ______________________

h supply ______________________

If the final *y* follows a vowel, you do not need to change the word—simply add the suffix.

For example: toy + *ed* = to**yed**
delay + *s* = dela**ys**

Activity 2

Modify the words in the table by adding the requested **suffixes**. The first one has been done for you.

Word	s/es	ing	ed
cry	cries	crying	cried
study			
toy			
party			
spy			
pay			
marry			

Activity 3

Complete the sentences below by using the correct **form** of the words in the box using the suffixes in the table you just completed.

grey beauty pretty dry theory defy apply worry

a The celebratory fireworks after the wedding reception were __________.

b My mother embraced her __________ hair as a sign of wisdom.

c The land was the __________ Kath Walker had ever seen it when she returned home.

d Martin Luther King didn't tell his wife about the threats; he didn't like __________ her.

e My father always has the craziest __________ about aliens and time-travel.

f Mr Jones was always __________ for scholarships to visit new and exotic places.

g Staring at her soft eyes, Cook knew she was the __________ thing he would ever see.

h Billy and Sam didn't mind __________ their mother; it was their father they were scared of.

Activity 4

Identify the spelling errors in the sentences below. Write the **correct spelling** of the incorrect word in the space provided.

a Martin sat hunched crying in his chair, enviing every moment Barry got to spend with Judy. __________

b Nelson Mandela was known for happily emploing the very poor. __________

c Mother Theresa spent every evening worrying about and praing for the souls of the sick and poor. __________

d Michelangelo is famous for his beautiful painting portraing the Last Judgment. __________

You be the teacher

Below is a **body paragraph** for a biography of a musician, written by a Year 8 student. There are some errors in the structure of the paragraph and the spelling of some of the words with **suffixes**. There are other spelling errors too. Rewrite the paragraph below with the **correct structure** and with the **correct spelling of all words**.

The best-selling single of his solo career was 'Imagine', a song with a hopful message for the future. At some point in his life, Lennon went solo. Lennon proved he was moore than just a Beatle—he was an artist. He was commended for his beautyful melodies and his envyable originality. Working as a solo muscician, Lennon composed well over one hundred songs.

Now you write

It is now time for you to complete a **biography** of your best friend.

1 Before you write, take some time to look at the student writing samples on the following pages as a guide to writing standards. Note the mistakes made in the Intermediate sample and try to avoid making these mistakes yourself.

2 Once you have read the two student writing samples, take some time to think about what you believe are the most important features of a biography that you need to master. Use the lines below to jot down your answer to this question:

What do you find most difficult when writing this kind of text?

3 Now look at the imaginative text marking criteria on page ix to double-check that you understand the requirements for a really good piece of imaginative writing.

Remember that you have already done your planning and drafted your introduction and conclusion. Use your own paper. Good luck!

Looking at other students' writing

Biographies:

Write a biography of your favourite musician.

Orientation
The student uses a strong orientation that grabs the reader's attention through the brief overview of what Lennon is best known for.

Narrative techniques
The language is formal and mostly objective. The biography is mostly written in the past tense.

Text structure
The biography is well structured, featuring a series of facts about Lennon's life in chronological order.

Paragraphing
A new paragraph is used when there is a change in time or place or a new event is introduced.

Cohesion
Connectives and conjunctions are used to indicate when events occurred (e.g. *furthermore, however* and *after*).

ADVANCED SAMPLE

BIOGRAPHY: John Lennon

John Lennon was one of the world's most popular musicians. He was originally acclaimed as a founding member of the rock and roll band, The Beatles. However, he became celebrated for his political activism. Lennon used his fame to promote peace and social causes that he felt were important.

Lennon was born in Liverpool, United Kingdom, in 1940. When he was 16 he met Paul McCartney and they formed a band, The Beatles, which would go on to change the face of music forever. When Lennon was 21, the band was signed to the record label, EMI. This was the beginning of his life as a famous musician.

Lennon became a husband and father in 1962 after he married Cynthia Powell. In 1964, The Beatles did their first tour of the United States and John Lennon became known all around the world. He enjoyed great success with the band, releasing many critically acclaimed albums and touring the world.

However, the late 1960s brought with it many changes for Lennon. He divorced Cynthia and remarried Japanese avant-garde artist, Yoko Ono. Furthermore, after struggling to deal with conflicting musical preferences, The Beatles finally broke up in 1969.

After the band's demise, Lennon proved he was more than just a Beatle—he was an artist. Working as a solo musician, Lennon composed well over one hundred songs. The best-selling single of his solo career was 'Imagine', a song with a hopeful message for the future. Lennon has been commended for his beautiful melodies and his enviable originality.

Tragically, John Lennon was shot and killed outside of his apartment complex in New York City on December 8th, 1980. It was later discovered that the killer was a crazed fan who was frustrated with how Lennon lived. Lennon's death was mourned by millions of music fans all around the world. His life is commemorated at the Strawberry Fields memorial in New York City's Central Park.

John Lennon's music continues to influence a new generation of singers and songwriters. He is remembered for his faith in a better world for all people but mostly he is remembered for being a musical genius.

Vocabulary
Difficult vocabulary is used. A variety of abstract nouns are used to enhance the recount (e.g. *activism, demise* and *preferences*).

Sentence structure
A variety of sentence lengths are used to avoid monotony and create interest. Complex sentences add detail.

Ideas
The subject of the biography (John Lennon) is developed and sustained throughout.

Punctuation
Correct punctuation is used. Complex punctuation is used where required.

Spelling
All words are spelt correctly. There is frequent inclusion of difficult or challenging words (e.g. *commended, avant-garde* and *mourning*).

Biographies:
Write a biography of your favourite musician.

Narrative techniques
The language is mostly formal and objective. In some places the biography is incorrectly written in the present tense (e.g. the third paragraph).

Sentence structure
The student attempts to use a variety of sentence lengths, but uses too many simple sentences (e.g. 'The band got famous quickly').

Opening
The student attempts to grab the reader's attention through a brief overview of Lennon's life but lacks the necessary details.

Paragraphing
A new paragraph is used to introduce a new event in Lennon's life.

Text structure
The student uses the correct structure of a biography but lacks detail (e.g. no dates for some events).

Cohesion
The biography is lacking connectives and conjunctions to indicate when events occurred.

INTERMEDIATE SAMPLE

BIOGRAPHY: John Lennon

John Lennon was a musician. He was originly known as a founding member of The Beatles, however later he was into politics. Lennon used his fame to promote things that he felt were important.

Lennon was born in Liverpool, United Kingdom, in 1940. When he was 16 he met Paul McCartney and they formed The Beatles, which a band. The band got famous quicklly.

Lennon gets married to Cynthia Powell and they had a son. The Beatles do a tour of the united states and john Lennon became known all around the world. He enjoys great success with the band, releasing popular songs.

The 1960s brought changes for Lennon! He got divorced and then married Yoko Ono. The Beatles broke up because they were struggeling to deal with conflicting musical tastes.

After the band broke up, Lennon went solo. lennon composed well over one hundred songs. The best-selling single of his solo career was 'Imagine' and Lennon has been commended for his great song writing!

John Lennon was shot and killed outside of his apartment complex in New York City. Many people were very sad about his death. There is a memorial to him called Strawberry Fields in New York City's Central Park.

John Lennon's music continues to influence a new singers and songwriters. He is remembered for his faith in a better world for all people and he is remembered for being a musical genius.

Ideas
Ideas are underdeveloped.

Punctuation
Correct punctuation is mostly used but there are some errors (e.g. capital letters missing for proper nouns).

Vocabulary
The student attempts to use abstract nouns and adverbs. They need to use more appropriate nouns (e.g. 'into politics' could be 'political activism'; 'tastes could be 'preferences').

Spelling
Most words are spelt correctly. Some words with suffixes are spelt incorrectly (e.g. 'struggeling' instead of *struggling*, 'originly' instead of *originally* and 'quicklly' instead of *quickly*).

Note: words shaded in blue are errors.

UNIT TWELVE

12

Imaginative texts
Narrative poems

Understanding the question

Compose a twelve-line narrative poem telling of an alien invasion of Earth.

Type of question

This question is asking you to write a particular type of imaginative text—a **narrative poem**.

A narrative poem is very much like a short story. Both attempt to **tell a tale in detail** and make it interesting for the reader.

Features of a narrative poem

* Aims to use the poetic form to tell a story and engage readers
* Has a title that tells what the poem is about
* Tells a story that typically has a beginning, middle and end
* Is divided into stanzas
* Each stanza contains a single image or event
* Language appeals to the mind, heart and senses
* Uses sound devices: regular rhyme scheme, alliteration, onomatopoeia
* Uses poetic devices to create images: alliteration, simile, metaphor

1 Write as many synonyms as you can for the **content words** below.

a alien ______________________

____

b invasion ______________________

____

c Earth ______________________

____

d narrative ______________________

____

2 Write three synonyms for the **task word** *compose*.

____

Writing a great poem takes many attempts. Don't be surprised if you spend a lot of time on your drafts!

Planning and organisation

A **narrative poem** is a long poem that tells a story. As you've seen in Unit 10 writing narratives can be tricky, so be prepared to spend time **planning** and **drafting** until you're happy with your final poem.

Activity 1

Use the table below to **brainstorm images** for your poem. Write as many things as you can about each aspect—be as creative as you want.

Alien invasion			
See	**Hear**	**Smell**	**Feel**

Activity 2

Using your own paper, write for 3 to 5 minutes without worrying about it being right or wrong. Write anything that comes into your head—don't stop! This is called **automatic writing**. At the end of this time, read back through your writing and circle any **images**, words or sentences that you like. Write these in the box. These will help you start your poem.

Activity 3

1 What are three **powerful** images you could create to show the aliens are threatening or peaceful (e.g. a scowling alien pointing angrily at a human child)?

2 What are three **powerful images** you could create to show that the people are scared or curious (e.g. a human child staring wide-eyed in wonder as the alien craft comes into view)?

Activity 4

You need to consider from whose perspective the story will be told.

Look back at **Unit 9** for more information on **narrative perspective**.

a What could you include if it is written in the **third person**?

For example: The women and children shuddered in fear.

b What could you include if it is written in the **first person**?

For example: I looked in my sister's eyes and they reflected my fear.

Structure

There isn't one correct way to **structure** a **narrative poem**. This is because there are so many different types of narratives. The ancient epic poem *The Iliad* by Homer is almost 16 000 lines long! For your narrative poem, you only need to write twelve lines and you can stick to the traditional narrative structure: **orientation**, **complication** and **resolution**.

Return to **Unit 10** to read more about the structure of **narratives**.

Stanzas

Most narrative poems are divided into paragraphs called **stanzas**. These are sometimes referred to as **verses**. Your narrative poem will consist of three stanzas—one stanza for each of the three main parts of your narrative. You may wish to add another stanza for the complication of the narrative.

Activity 1

Plot is important to a narrative poem and you will look at it more closely in the next section of this unit. For now, try to complete the table.

Plot part	Thinking questions	Your poem
Orientation	* What mood is this beginning? (e.g. happy, sad, anxious, scared) * What action takes place at the beginning of your story? (e.g. how the aliens arrive and people's reaction to them) * What images will you include to communicate this to your reader?	
Complication	* What is the main mood of the middle of the story? * What action takes place in the middle of your story? * What images will you include to communicate this to your reader?	
Resolution	* What is the main mood at the end of the story? * What action takes place at the end of your story? * What images will you include to communicate this to your reader?	

Activity 2

Draft the opening stanza of your poem. Try to **capture the emotions** and senses of an alien invasion. Use your notes taken during the organisation stage on page 136.

Language feature

Poetic devices

Narrative poems make great **use of sound** to engage the reader in the story being told. Sound devices such as **alliteration**, **onomatopoeia**, **assonance** and **rhyme** work together to **build characters**, **setting** and **action**.

Alliteration

Alliteration is the repetition of the **same consonant sounds** at the beginning of words in a line of poetry.

For example: The **l**ovely **l**ady **l**eaned her perfumed head on my **l**onely shoulder.

Activity 1

Choose words from the box to create **alliteration** in the lines of poetry below. The first one has been done for you.

dark	lean	hugged	clattered	sparks	red

a She was all dark black hair and bright ___red___ ribbons as she sauntered into the room.

b The wolf's ________________ dreadful eyes lingered in my mind.

c Lanky and ________________, Jim the sports star wowed his fans.

d I touched his arm; ________________ shot through me.

e The door clanged and ________________ as the wind caught it.

f An inhuman hush ________________ the crowd of onlookers.

Activity 2

Add **alliterative adjectives** to draw attention to the main noun in these lines of poetry. The first one has been done for you.

a She crept inside the ___curious___ cave.

b The ________________ lady sat in despair.

c The ________________ boy was sent to his room.

d The ________________ witch cackled at the scared child.

e Creeping up behind his prey, the ________________ lion pounced.

f The ________________ ants irritated the little girl.

Onomatopoeia

Onomatopoeia is the use of words that **sound like** the sound they're trying to capture.

For example: The **snap** of the twigs.

Activity 3

Match the object/people/animals with their **sounds** below. The first one has been done for you.

a	a door closing	rumble
b	a cat	drip
c	an angry person	crash
d	a leaky tap	meow
e	a wave	squeak
f	a mouse	bellows
g	an empty stomach	bang

Activity 4

Complete the lines of poetry by adding the appropriate **onomatopoeia** from the box.

whooped groaning squeaked swish trickle mumbled

a She walked light as a fairy and ______________________ like a mouse.

b I was soothed by the sounds of the children as they ______________________ in their sleep.

c The wind thrashed violently against the ______________________ window panes.

d Seven silent fish ______________________ across a canopy of rainbows.

e The river was just a ______________________ and I sighed in disappointment.

f Parrots ______________________ through the golden sky; I was in paradise.

Assonance

Assonance is the deliberate grouping together of words with **similar vowel sounds**. The purpose of this technique is to give **emphasis** to certain words. It also creates a musical effect, similar to rhyme.

For example: The cr**u**mbling th**u**nder of seas.

Activity 5

Underline the words that have the same vowel sounds (**assonance**) in these lines of poetry.

a 'Soft language issued from their spitless lips.' (James Joyce)

b 'Hear the mellow wedding bells.' (Edgar Allen Poe)

c 'Strips of tinfoil winking like people.' (Sylvia Plath)

Activity 6

Go back to the planning section where you listed all of the **sounds** you would hear during an alien invasion. List them in the space below. Try to think of words that link to these sounds which share a **similar vowel sound**.

For example: *crack* has a similar vowel sound to *thwack*.

Activity 7

Go back to the draft of your opening stanza that you wrote earlier. Take some time to redraft your stanza, adding in **alliteration**, **onomatopoeia** and **assonance** where appropriate.

Rhyme

Rhyme gives a poem a **musical quality** and makes it easier to be read and remembered. Poems are like songs—they are meant to be heard. When you're writing your poem, take time to **read the lines out loud** to hear what they sound like. This will especially help when adding rhyme. Narrative poems are more likely to rhyme than other poems as they are often performed and read for an audience.

Words rhyme when they **share a similar sound**, such as *fly* and *sky*. In your poem, try to include end-of-line rhyme. This is where two words with the same sounds come at the end of a pair of lines. A pair of rhyming lines is called a **couplet**. Here is an example of end-of-line rhyme from Alfred Noyes's narrative poem 'The Highwayman'. The rhyming words have been highlighted for you.

> The wind was a torrent of darkness among the gusty **trees**,
> The moon was a ghostly galleon tossed upon cloudy **seas**,

Activity 8

How many **rhyming words** can you think of for these words? Try to make the list as long as possible!

sky	fright	delay	crack

Activity 9

Use words from the box to complete the **couplets** below.

snow	fire	lights	me	form

a The sun touched my face and I felt suddenly warm,
My lips curled into the grandest smile I could ______________________.

b Down beneath the bridge, I can see
Two impish children laughing at ______________________.

c Mr Madness has eyes like ______________________,
I wonder what he does desire.

d He darted dangerously away from the flashing ______________________,
Knowing full well the police had him in their sights,

e No sign of an end to the beating ______________________,
Snuggle down and enjoy the wintery show.

Activity 10

From the lists in Activities 8 and 9, list **rhyming pairs** of words that you might use in your own narrative poem.

____

____

____

____

____

____

Activity 11

Go back to the draft of your opening stanza again. Take some time to redraft your stanza, adding in a **regular rhyme scheme**. Remember that in poetry, the organisation of words in a line of poetry does not need to look like a normal sentence. Sometimes words might find themselves in unusual places.

____

____

____

____

____

____

Activity 12

Here is an example of a stanza written by a student for a narrative poem about a shark attack.

The Shark
The dark deep surrounds me, like an ice vice
and my heart lurches and groans.
I sense it before I see it; the monster of the deep
who wants my bones.

a In your own words, explain what the student wants us to **see** when he describes the shark as *the monster of the deep.*

b Write down an image the student uses to make us **feel** that the water is cold.

c Find one example of **alliteration**. In your own words explain why it has been used.

d Write the words from the stanza that most **convey the fear** of the swimmer.

Spotlight *on spelling*

Homophones

Homophones are words that **sound alike** but have **different spellings** and **meanings**. It is very easy to confuse these words. Homophones were briefly covered in Unit 8.

lesson/lessen	lightening/lightning
sea/see	canvas/canvass
chilli/chilly	paste/paced
cited/sighted	scents/sense
ceiling/sealing	presence/presents
pain/pane	pray/prey
passed/past	profit/prophet
bear/bare	board/bored
breaking/braking	

Activity 1

Find words from the **homophone pairs** on the previous page that answer the following. Use your dictionary if needed. The first one has been done for you.

a a person gifted with profound moral insight and exceptional powers of expression
prophet

b an abrupt, discontinuous natural electric discharge in the atmosphere

____

c plant bearing very hot and finely tapering long peppers; usually red ________________

d an animal hunted or caught for food ________________

e to examine carefully or discuss thoroughly ________________

f uninterested because of frequent exposure or indulgence ________________

Activity 2

Complete the following sentences with the correct **forms** of words from the previous word list.

a You are not the only person who will ________________ from this deal.

b I could hear her heart ________________ as I told her we were over.

c Jennifer was only interested in ________________ the tips of her hair.

d Spending more time with Mum didn't ________________ the pain of not seeing Dad.

e I had to spend three boring hours ________________ envelopes.

f Janie said the pain of losing her dog was too hard to ________________.

Activity 3

Underline the correct word in each of the following sentences.

a Only out in the deep, deep ocean I can (sea/see) my true self.

b Hundreds of years have (passed/past) and yet I still long to be human.

c Under the ruined staircase is hidden a secret, magical (board/bored).

d Without glancing up, I could (sense/scents) he was here with me.

e Threatened and afraid, he (paced/paste) the worn carpet.

f My neck cracked and I groaned in (pain/pane).

Activity 4

Choose three of the words from the box on the previous page and use each in a separate line to help you with your narrative poem about the invading aliens.

a ____

b ____

c ____

You be the teacher

Below is a **stanza** for a narrative poem written by a year 8 student. There are some errors in the structure of the lines in the stanza and some confusion with **homophones**. There is one other spelling error as well. Rewrite the stanza so the **narrative makes sense** and with the **correct spelling of all words**.

I began to experience a most unusual and unearthly feeling.
The lightening was a jagged rod of anger across the sky,
Staring up at that darkined and ominous Earthly sealing,
The thunder screamed in banging bursts away so high.

Now you write

It is time for you to complete your own **narrative poem** about an alien invasion.

1 Before you write, take some time to look at the student writing samples on the following pages as a guide to writing standards. Note the mistakes made in the Intermediate sample and try to avoid making these mistakes yourself.

2 Once you have read the two student writing samples, take some time to think about what you believe are the most important features of a narrative poem that you need to master. Use the lines below to jot down your answer to this question:

What do you find most difficult when writing this kind of text?

3 Now look at the imaginative text marking criteria on page ix to double-check that you understand the requirements for a really good piece of narrative writing.

Remember that you have already done your planning and drafted some of your stanzas. Use your own paper. Good luck!

Looking at other students' writing

Narrative poems:

Write a poem that tells the story of a shark attack.

Orientation
There is a strong orientation that grabs the reader's attention through the use of figurative language.

Narrative techniques
The student uses descriptive language to engage the reader's imagination and emotions.

Sound devices such as alliteration and onomatopoeia are used well.

Cohesion
There is continuity of ideas throughout the description; the focus is always on the shark attack.

ADVANCED SAMPLE

SHARK ATTACK

Pristine. Remote. Best spot on the coast. The waves are why I come.
They curve clear arcs in the sunlight and beat the sand like a drum.
The dark deep surrounds me, my heart lurches and groans.
I sense it before I see it, the monster who wants my bones.

I'm the legend of the ocean. The one no one likes to see.
My body is plated with steel; crunching ice vice teeth for me.
Once you're in my deadly sight, I'll never let you go.
Brutal, bloody and barbaric, I put on quite a show.

Rumours reported screams for help and failed heroes hanging heads.
Fresh shark sightings held even the bravest to their beds.
The beach was closed at sunset. The sad vigil went throughout the night.
But the fearless big wave surfer never came back into sight.

Vocabulary
Difficult vocabulary is used. A variety of adjectives and strong verbs are used to enhance the images created (e.g. *lurches* and *crunching*).

Sentence structure
A variety of sentence lengths are used to avoid monotony and create interest. Short and one-word sentences create drama.

Ideas
The theme of the narrative poem (a shark attack) is developed and sustained throughout.

Punctuation
Correct punctuation is used. Complex punctuation is used where required.

Text structure
The narrative poem is well structured, featuring obvious orientation, complication and resolution. It also cleverly uses three different perspectives to tell the story of the shark attack.

Paragraphing
A new stanza is used to introduce a main part of the poem's narrative and a new speaker's perspective. Tension is built effectively.

Spelling
All words are spelt correctly. There is frequent inclusion of difficult or challenging words (e.g. *fearless*, *vigil* and *barbaric*).

Narrative poems:

Write a poem that tells the story of a shark attack.

Opening
The student attempts to grab the reader's attention through the use of intrigue. The writing lacks emotion.

Narrative techniques
There is some use of descriptive language to engage the reader's imagination and emotions. There are simplistic attempts at figurative language (e.g. *my heart starts to groan*).

Sentence structure
The student attempts to use a variety of sentence lengths.

Paragraphing
A new paragraph is used to introduce a new idea about a shark.

Text structure
The student uses the correct structure of a narrative poem but lacks detail.

INTERMEDIATE SAMPLE

SHARK ATTACK

Pretty remote. best spot on the coast. The waves are why I come.
They are blue and sound noisy like a drum.
The water is around me and my heart starts to groan.
Because I have scene a shark and it wants my bones.

I'm the scaryest thing in the ocean and no one likes me.
I'm scary because I have big scary teeth ... in my mouth.
Once your in my deadly sight, I'll never let you go.
I'm really scary and aggressive. I will rip you to pieces.

People say they heard someone screaming but no one helped.
fear of being attacked kept even the bravest in their beds.
The beach was closed at sunset. the sad waiting went throughhout the night.
But the brave big wave surfer never came back into sight.

Ideas
The student touches on the theme of the description (a shark attack) throughout. The ideas are underdeveloped.

Punctuation
The student mostly uses correct punctuation. There are some errors (e.g. capital letters missing and misuse of ellipsis).

Cohesion
There is continuity of ideas throughout the short story. The student uses repetitive line beginnings that do not add impact (e.g. *I'm* in the third stanza).

Vocabulary
The student attempts to use a variety of adjectives and strong verbs but needs to use more interesting words (e.g. *brave* could be *fearless*; *pretty* could be *pristine*).

Spelling
Most words are spelt correctly. Some homophones are spelt incorrectly (e.g. 'scene' instead of *seen* and 'your' instead of *you're*).

Note: words shaded in blue are errors.

Selected answers

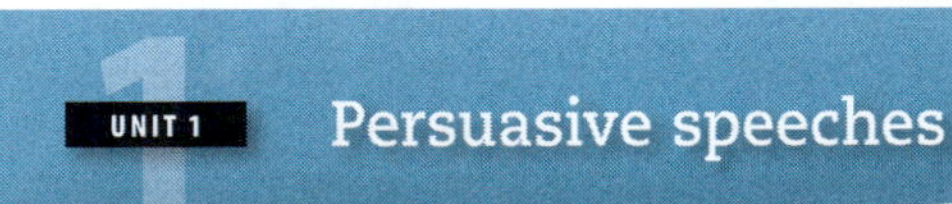

UNIT 1 Persuasive speeches

Understanding the question page 1

1
- **a** a device containing gunpowder and other combustible chemicals that causes a spectacular explosion when ignited
- **b** officially or legally prohibited
- **c** intended for private use or use by one person

Writing skills pages 4–7

1

a statistic	Why didn't the chicken cross the road? Because it was afraid of the fireworks.
b rhetorical question	There's no use denying it, the end of the world is coming.
c joke	Infant mortality for Indigenous Australians is three times that of other Australians.
d statement	When was the last time you thought about the feelings of the animal on the end of your fork?

3 Removing meat from your diet can not only save you, but it could save the world. Did you know that in the United States approximately 41 million tonnes of plant protein is fed to livestock each year? Growing this plant protein requires large amounts of water and energy—things our world has in short supply.

To protect the health of our planet it is clear that we must stop eating meat.

Language feature pages 7–8

1
- **b** CERTAIN **c** CERRTAIN
- **d** UNCERTAIN **e** UNCERTAIN

2
- **a** might **b** must
- **c** Perhaps/could **d** should absolutely never

3
- **a** Perhaps Australian politicians should not allow fireworks to be legalised for personal use.
- **b** Maybe fireworks could be sold with a warning label.

Spotlight on spelling page 9

1
- **a** certainly **b** definitely **c** hopefully
- **d** frequently **e** entirely

2
- **a** possibly **b** responsibly **c** arguably
- **d** abominably **e** ably

3
- **a** ordinarily **b** happily **c** angrily
- **d** compulsorily **e** derogatorily

You be the teacher page 10

Correct structure: One reason that fireworks definitely shouldn't be banned in Australia is because they provide parents with an opportunity to teach children valuable lessons about explosives. Fireworks are amazingly beautiful, however, they can be dangerous if children attempt to use them without parental guidance. Clearly the beauty of fireworks brings families together in a learning experience. This is one reason why I believe fireworks must be permitted for personal use in Australia.

Unnecessary sentence: When was the last time you looked up in the evening sky to discover brilliant colours and shapes?

Spelling errors: reason, definitely, amazingly, clearly

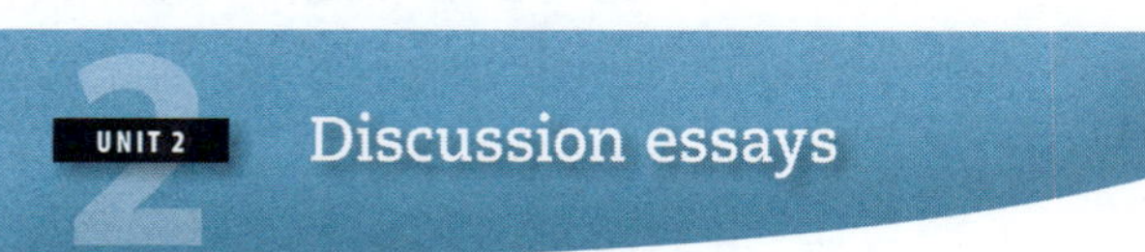

UNIT 2 Discussion essays

Understanding the question page 13

1
- **a** discuss **b** define **c** compare
- **d** outline **e** evaluate **f** explain
- **g** discuss **h** illustrate **i** write

Structure pages 15–17

1 Correct order of sentences:
- **b** Mobile phones have been part of our lives for the last 20 years.

c Since the late 1990s, Australians have been able to send text messages via their mobile phones and text messaging is now so popular that some young people send more than 100 texts per day.

a Some people believe that we should spend less time text messaging but others feel that we do not need to limit the number of texts we send.

3 Some people believe that aliens exist and visit our planet. (1) In 2012, thousands of people attended the 21st annual International UFO Congress. (2) This conference had speakers from all over the world and people spent their time discussing their personal encounters with aliens as well as their theories about UFOs. (3) From the large number of attendees at this conference, it is clear that many people do believe that aliens exist and visit our planet. (4)

5 The existence of aliens is disputed by many people, but some people believe that aliens exist and visit our planet. (1) After considering both points of view it is obvious that there is limited credible evidence to support alien sightings and therefore it is highly unlikely that aliens have visited our planet. (2) Therefore, in my view, aliens do not exist. (3)

Language feature pages 18–19

1
- a in summary
- b conversely
- c lastly
- d in contrast
- e to conclude
- f consequently
- g otherwise
- h thus
- i alternatively
- j nevertheless
- k on the other hand
- l however

2
- a Yet
- b Yet
- c However
- d Alternatively

3 a However b Yet c In contrast

Spotlight on spelling pages 19–20

1
a zeroes b ghettoes c mementoes
d torpedoes e embargoes f jellies
g eyelashes h flashes i theories
j studies k families l leashes
m gashes n absurdities o accessories
p activities q capabilities r certainties
s libraries t countries u faculties
v allergies w approaches x attachments
y dispatches z trenches

2
a speeches b heroes c countries
d animals e absurdities f theories
g tornadoes h supplies

You be the teacher page 21

Correct structure: Some people believe that zoos are not cruel. Zoos in cities do good work because they protect animals from poachers who wish to harm the animals. Many animals in the wild are at risk of being hunted and killed by poachers. Consequently it is understandable why some people believe that zoos are not cruel because they may act as sanctuaries for endangered animals.

Spelling errors: sanctuaries, zoos, cities, animals, poachers

UNIT 3 Film reviews

Understanding the question pages 24–25

1 a formal assessment or examination of something OR to think about critically or examine closely (Answers will vary.)

2 Film might refer to motion pictures or the industry that makes motion pictures. Films usually tell stories using moving pictures and audio.

3 An animated feature film is a film that features cartoons, claymation or digital drawings to tell stories. Often animation is created using a frame-by-frame technique.

4 Children are the target audience for most animated films because these films tend to have humorous or fairy-tale style narratives, which attract a younger audience.

Structure pages 27–29

2 Correct order for paragraph:

b *The Hunger Games* was directed by Gary Ross and was released into cinemas on March 22nd 2012.

a The film is based on the first book of the series *The Hunger Games* by author Suzanne Collins.

d The film has been hotly anticipated by fans of Suzanne Collins' highly acclaimed *The Hunger Games* trilogy.

c It was well adapted by the director and the actors were very well selected to suit the characters.

4 Unnecessary sentences: 2 and 4

Language feature pages 29–30

1
- a absurdly
- b annoyingly
- c aimlessly
- d Curiously
- e disappointingly

2
a inexplicably b luckily
c brilliantly d oddly

3 a a hoard of wild monkeys let loose in your living room
b her ten-thousandth sigh
c I don't think a jet plane would be able to keep up
d you can occasionally see a hundred-dollar bill fall from the screen

4 a Keira Knightley and a toothpick. She is very thin.
b George Clooney and the hills. He is old.
c Daniel Radcliffe and knight in shining armour. He is heroic and handsome.

Spotlight on spelling pages 31–32

1 b irrational c impossible
d irregular e irrelevant
f irreverent g irresistible
h unafraid i unaffordable
j unbroken k unexcited
l ungrateful m unimaginative
n unintelligent o inactive
p debrief

2 a unintelligent b deconstruct
c impossible d irrational

3 b sublet c subdivide
d subscribe e embody
f disable g disbelieve
h disconnect i disappear
j embalm k disclose
l implant m embrace
n impale o disfigure
p embed q disapprove
r disappoint

4 a disapprove b disbelieve
c disconnect d subscribe

You be the teacher page 33

Correct structure: The action sequences in *The Incredibles* are nothing short of incredible. The director cleverly contrasts the uninteresting domestic life of the Parr family with the thrills and danger of the superhero life. While it lacks the gimmick factor of the big 3D films, it certainly doesn't lack action and plot. It's impossible not to be carried along with Mr Incredible as he attempts to live a double life and relive his glory days as a superhero.
Spelling errors: incredible, certainly, cleverly, uninteresting, impossible

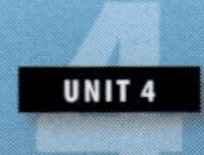

UNIT 4 Blog posts

Understanding the question page 36

1 a Reality television features ordinary people in ordinary situations or situations to create conflict. It has no scripts or actors. (Answers will vary.)
b to overestimate the merits of; rate too highly

2 overestimate, overvalue

Structure pages 38–39

1

a statement	i firmly believe that reading a book is far superior to watching television.
b statistic	Young people between 8 to 18 years of age spend nearly 4 hours a day in front of a television screen.
c joke	What type of building has the most stories? A library!
d anecdote	Yesterday, for five hours solid, I was held captive on my lounge—I couldn't put my books down!
e rhetorical question	Who wouldn't love to spend every waking hour reading a book?

2 It's impossible to get quality pizza in Australia!
Once I had believed that our pizza was satisfying but last year I travelled to New York City and my appreciation for this take-away favourite was altered forever. Coming home to Oz, I've discovered that there are a few things that Australian pizza must work on: size, crust and toppings.

4

a quote	One of my favourite quotes about writing is by George Orwell who said, 'Writing a book is a horrible, exhausting struggle, like a long bout of some painful illness.'
b personal observation	People seem to be passionate about writing; if they weren't we wouldn't have all of the wonderful books in our libraries.
c anecdote	Just yesterday my little brother attempted to write his first story—it was only four jumbled words—but he was so excited with his work!

Language feature page 40

1

a pizza	How can we continue to live our lives as though there is no suffering in this world?
b mobile phones	When was the last time you took a really good look in your wardrobe?
c school	Could you live for three days without texting?
d poverty	Why can't Australians make a good pizza?
e fashion	Is it possible to enjoy a single day of school?

2 Examples of possible answers:

- b When will people start taking recycling seriously?
- c Wouldn't it be great if dogs cleaned up after themselves?
- d Don't you think it's time parents started playing video games too?

3 a Is it possible that … b Did you know …
c Isn't it about time that … d Should …

Spotlight on spelling pages 41–42

1 a theses b formula/formulae
c oases d stimuli
e curricula/curriculums

2 a media b diagnoses c axes
d analyses e foci/focuses f sheep
g data h synopses

3

Singular noun	Plural noun
index	indices
beau	beaux
crisis	crises
cactus	cacti
medium	media

You be the teacher pages 42–43

Correct structure: Don't you think it odd that we would sit for hours and hours watching other everyday people cook, clean, sing, dance or paint a house?
Our fixation with reality television is one of Australia's biggest cultural crises. Australia has some extremely talented creative artists—screenwriters, actors, designers—who could fill our screens with wonderfully fictitious television series and films. I just hope that Australians overcome this reality obsession soon.
I spend enough time in reality with all of its boring and messy bits.
Spelling errors: crises, screens, series

Understanding the question page 46

1 a series of actions conducted in a certain order or manner

2 Answers could include:
a changing a car tyre b writing a story
c making tacos d washing a car
e washing a dog

Structure page 49

3 Correct order: e, f, b, c, a, d

Language feature pages 51–52

1 a Divide, brush b Illustrate
c Present d Download, save
e stir f slice

2

- b While holding the dog steady, pour water onto its fur.
- c After brushing well, spit the toothpaste into the sink.
- d Before lighting the Bunsen burner, check the gas is working.
- e While holding down the command and function keys, press delete.
- f Once you have eaten your meal, clear the dishes away.
- g After you have swept the floors, prepare the soapy water for mopping.
- h Whileyour partner whisks the eggs, check the oven is fully preheated.
- i While the cake is in the oven, make the icing.
- j After buttering your toast, smear on the Vegemite.

Spotlight on spelling pages 52–54

1 a per-spec-tive b pre-sen-ta-tion
c pro-ces-sor d class-if-i-ca-tion
e ex-pla-na-tion f e-val-u-ate

2 Possible answers b microorganism
c bicycle d biology e psychology
f hyperactive g posthumous h intercept

You be the teacher page 54

Correct structure:

1 First, wash the dog's face.
2 Be careful not to get shampoo into its eyes are they are very sensitive.
3 Wash under the dog's legs.

4 Make sure you check for parasites like ticks when you do this.
5 After you have given the dog a good wash with shampoo, rinse its fur with water until all suds are removed.
6 Finally, when you've washed the dog you can let it shake its fur to remove excess water.

Spelling errors: excess, parasites

UNIT 6 Research reports

Understanding the question pages 58–59

1 carry out research or study so as to discover facts or information

2 to record something in writing

3 young people, music, research, findings

4 investigate systematically

5 an account given of a particular matter, usually after an investigation

6 Answers could include: book report, school report, news report.

Planning and organisation page 59

1 **a** closed **b** open **c** open
d open **e** closed

Structure pages 61–64

2

Question	Method
What effect does violence in the media have on teen crime?	internet/library research
What are Shakespeare's most common character types?	interviews
What impact does global warming have on our environment and our health?	internet/library research
Why do the elderly enjoy gardening?	survey
Who are our community's biggest polluters?	survey

3 Paragraph **b** is better. Reasons for this choice include more detail regarding number of participants, more detail about number and types of questions on the survey, and no vague language like *maybe more*, *some questions*, etc.

5 **a** 4 **b** 1 **c** 2 **d** 3

7 Paragraph **b** is better. Reasons for this choice include more formal and objective language and greater detail.

8

	Aim	Discussion
a	To measure the amount of non-recyclable rubbish in local primary schools.	Primary schools discard far too much non-recyclable rubbish.
b	To discover which brand of detergent is most popular between two varieties.	The non-name detergent is considered lesser quality and less likely to be used.
c	To determine the influence that sun safety commercials have on children aged 5 to 10.	Sun safety commercials have a significant effect on younger children aged 5 to 10.
d	To discover the impact that moving house has on teenagers.	Moving house is a traumatic experience for teenagers.
e	To determine if soft drink or fruit juice is more popular with young men aged 18 to 30.	Young men aged 18 to 30 are almost five times more likely to drink soft drink.
f	To determine how many objects a person can track at one time.	People can track up to four objects moving at moderate speed at any one time.

9 **a** results **b** method **c** results
d aim **e** method

Language feature page 65

1 **a** A **b** A **c** P
d P **e** A **f** P

2 **b** Data was collected over three weeks.
c The rubbish was counted by the students.
d Soft drink was preferred by the young men.
e The commercials were watched three times by the children.
f Moving house is not enjoyed by teenagers.

Spotlight on spelling pages 66–67

1 **b** unsurprisingly **c** inaccessible
d degrading **e** decomposing
f destabilised

2 **a** destitution **b** perfection
c tasteless **d** irrelevant
e transplant **f** unfinished

3 **a** sur-vey-ing **b** or-i-gin-ate
c in-vest-i-gate **d** in-ter-view-ees
e per-sis-tent **f** oc-cur-rence

You be the teacher pages 67–68

Correct structure: Ten boys and ten girls were included in this experiment. All participants were aged between 10 and 14 years. The participants were randomly selected using a criteria relating to socioeconomic status, age and gender. Participants were asked a series of ten questions about their use of video games. Survey questions related to frequency of gaming, accessibility to gaming consoles and game preferences.
Spelling errors: accessibility, preferences, experiment, participants

UNIT 7 Explanatory essays

Understanding the question page 71

1 to clearly outline; show how or why

2 **a** Explain **b** Discuss **c** Argue

Planning and organisation page 73

2 **b** Write an essay explaining the differences between cats.

Structure pages 74–76

1 (possible answer)

Children and teenagers sometimes feel that their parents are too strict; however, there are reasons for parents being strict. One of the more common explanations for why parents are strict is because parents are scared for the safety and wellbeing of their children. Another valid reason for parents being strict is that they wish to educate their children about the importance of respect and self-control. Finally, parents may be strict simply because they have more life experience and have a better understanding of appropriate behaviours.

3 **b** pollution in ABC Town **c** fixing a bicycle tyre **d** growing up in a small town **e** student success

4 conclusion two

Language feature page 77

1
- **a** Helping parents around the house can mean they stress less and more available to spend time with their children.
- **b** Parents are strict because they care a lot about their children.
- **c** Mowing the lawn once a week is an example of a job that can help parents out.
- **d** Some parents pay their children to help around the house.
- **e** Packing away things after they have been used can help parents as they have less tidying.

Spotlight on spelling page 78

1
- **a** amusement **b** abduction
- **c** eviction **d** advancement
- **e** commandment **f** terrorism
- **g** criticism **h** evidence
- **i** relation **j** happiness

2

Verb	Noun
equip	equipment
refresh	refreshment
involve	involvement
develop	development
infect	infection
connect	connection

You be the teacher pages 78–79

Correct structure: Assistance with washing up after dinner is just one way that children can help their parents out at home. Organisation and care is required during this activity, as there is the potential to break crockery. Washing up takes no longer than twenty minutes and can be made quicker if someone else does the drying up. Children should do the washing up every night after dinner because this helps their parents a lot.
Spelling errors: organisation, potential, assistance

UNIT 8 News reports

Understanding the question page 82

1
- **a** noteworthy information about recent or important events
- **b** an account given of a particular matter

2 Answers could include: **a** bank robbery **b** death of a celebrity **c** bushfires **d** new prime minister **e** teacher strike

Structure pages 84–87

1 Local river is polluted by paint factory: Red River Rage
Car accident in busy shopping mall: Car Ploughs Through Mall
Man saves his dog from drowning in surf: Man Saves Best Friend
Football team wins grand final: Eagles Win Cup

2 Answers could include:
- **a** Stallion enjoys sun and surf
- **b** 100 years of learning
- **c** A 5-star dinner
- **d** Holiday makers amazed by jellyfish
- **e** Three's not a crowd at local shopping centre

5 **a** neighbours, occupants, firefighters
b police, Woolworths manager, parents

6 Sentences that are too long:
The locals have started playing classical music loudly through car speakers and throwing large bones for the dogs to eat but this has enraged some dog owners but some are happy with the moves.
The actions have come as a surprise to the dog owners but one of the owners commented that 'This was like Christmas for our dogs and we hope it continues'. and another observed that they had not noticed the dogs barking.
Extra point in second paragraph: The dogs in the street range from small Chihuahuas to a big Rottweiler.

7 c is the better selection because it provides an indication on the outcome of the event being reported on.

Language feature page 88

1 **a** subjective **b** objective
c objective **d** subjective

2 Answers could include:
- **a** The temperatures were high when the fire spread through the town.
- **b** Constable Black stated, 'This is a tragedy for the Bluelake Community.'
- **c** Mr Anstley accepted his award for heroism.
- **d** The badly damaged boat was dragged into the harbour by the coast guards.

3 Answers could include:
- **a** In Australia there are large penalties for littering.
- **b** At the time of the accident most people were asleep in their beds.
- **c** The Sydney 2000 Olympics were good for Australian sport and spirit.
- **d** The New Zealand Prime Minister wore a silver skirt and white blouse.
- **e** Many people in the community don't support the policies of the local government.

Spotlight on spelling pages 89–91

1

Noun	Verb
advice	advise
device	devise
practice	practise
licence	license

2 **a** practise (verb) **b** licence (noun)
c advice (noun) **d** device (noun)

3 **a** you're **b** it's **c** your
d their **e** whether **f** where

4 **a** effect **b** lose **c** than
d affect **e** then **f** loss

You be the teacher page 91

Correct structure: Bank robbers have broken into a bank in North Riverdale, police say. The robbery took place at approximately 3 am. The crime was discovered when the bank manager arrived for work, noticed the front glass doors were open slightly and saw a lot of broken glass inside the entryway. It's believed there were no witnesses to the robbery. A police spokesperson said the robbers left behind DNA evidence which was being used to further their investigation.
Spelling errors: were, it's, there, were, their

UNIT 9 Descriptions

Understanding the question page 95

1 frequented by a ghost

2 abode, dwelling, homestead

3 to write or create

Planning and organisation pages 98–99

4 **b** (possible answer)

From where I stood, the box looked normal.
I stared at it for just a moment before I began to unwrap its crackly brown paper and loosely tied string. My heart raced with my excitement. Underneath the boring surface of the box was something far more interesting—a shiny red container emblazoned with foreign-looking symbols. Poking my nose close to the jagged black symbols, I could hardly believe my eyes.

d (possible answer)

Jill looked up just in time to see the small black shapes begin to cloud the sky. These were like nothing she had ever seen before. Clearly they were some form of craft as they hovered together in a large, dark semicircle. Her eyes squinted into small slits as she stared, mouth open, at the sky. A small glistening bead of sweat trickled down her neck and she began to clench her fists.

Structure page 100

3 Correct order of sentences: d, a, b, c, f, e

Language feature pages 100–103

1 Answers will vary.

2 Answers will vary.

3 a metaphor b personification c simile

4 a aural b visual
c aural d visual

5 a short sentences b questions
c exclamations d questions, exclamations
e questions f exclamations
g short sentences

Spotlight on spelling pages 104–106

1

Noun	Adjective
accept	acceptable
comfort	comfortable
desire	desirable
cure	cureable
memory	memorial
perceive	perceivable
shake	shakable
value	valuable
unspoken	unspeakable

2 Sentences will vary. Adjectives:
b elegant c irrelevant
d significant e arrogant
f resistant g tolerant

3

Noun	Adjective
hilarity	hilarious
anxiety	anxious
glory	glorious
luxury	luxurious
space	spacious
variety	various
infection	infectious
fury	furious
deviant	devious
contagion	contagious

You be the teacher pages 106–107

Correct structure: The setting sun threw glorious streaks of red and orange across the darkening sky and the air felt thick with smoke. I wondered if I had the wrong address because this house looked much too big and far too old. The house loomed ahead like a giant beast and I began to feel very uncomfortable. Dark windows stared into my anxious mind. My lungs refused to take in the unfriendly air and I found myself wheezing and aching to be anywhere but here.
Spelling errors: glorious, uncomfortable, anxious

UNIT 10 Short stories

Understanding the question pages 110–111

1 to summarise the main ideas of the story

2 a violent collision

3 fracture, fragment, smash, shatter, collision

Structure pages 113–115

1 a action b in a car/on the road
c Aziz d intrigue
e Mars f Kalini

Language feature pages 115–117

1 Answers may include:
b scurry c prattle d grin
e caress f lob g sob
h cackle i exclaim j leap

2 Answers may include:
b *Neighbours* c Dee Why d Converse
e Ford f mansion g *Twilight*
h *Harry Potter* i singlet j iPhone

3 Answers will vary.

Spotlight on spelling pages 118–119

1

Root word	Present tense	Past tense
bath	bathing	bathed
purchase	purchasing	purchased
dance	dancing	danced
rebel	rebelling	rebelled
extend	extending	extended
hope	hoping	hoped
reverse	reversing	reversed
mix	mixing	mixed

Root word	Present tense	Past tense
resign	resigning	resigned
examine	examining	examined
exercise	exercising	exercised
confront	confronting	confronted
prop	propping	propped
admit	admitting	admitted
permit	permitting	permitted

2
a hastily
b swiftly
c surely
d horizontally
e stealthily
f successfully
g thirdly
h publicly
i critically
j unconsciously
k hopefully
l aggressively
m sunnily
n awkwardly
o ideally
p breezily
q technically
r originally
s subtly
t undeniably
u truly
v decisively

You be the teacher pages 119–120

Correct structure: A strong smell of petrol slowly filled the air and Jai felt his head spin.
Pushing on the orange button, Jai tried once again to release himself from the seatbelt. It was stuck. Getting out of the car immediately was all Jai had been able to think of and now he found himself trapped.
Looking desperately to his left his eye caught sight of a bright red cylinder. The fire extinguisher! It was his only hope, but could he reach it?
Spelling errors: slowly, desperately, immediately

UNIT 11 Biographies

Understanding the question page 123

1 a written account of a person's life; the study of lives of individuals

Structure pages 125–127

1 Order of sentences: b, a, d, c

4 Order of information: d, b, c, a

5
b Shakespeare enjoyed making his audience laugh. (He) often included clowns just for this purpose.

c After winning gold at the 2000 Olympic Games, Cathy Freeman draped (herself) with the Aboriginal flag. This caused outrage because unofficial flags are banned from the Olympic Games.

d Keira Knightly is one of the most popular female actresses today. (She) has been nominated for many acting awards during (her) career.

Language feature page 129

1
a Then
b Finally
c Eventually
d Thirdly
e Eventually
f Meanwhile

2
a Meanwhile
b Since then
c Until then
d Next

3 However, Finally

Spotlight on spelling pages 130–131

1
a enjoyed
b applied
c stayed
d tried
e played
f tidied
g delayed
h supplied

2

Word	s/es	ing	ed
cry	cries	crying	cried
study	studies	studying	studied
toy	toys	toying	toyed
party	parties	partying	partied
spy	spies	spying	spied
pay	paying	pays	paid
marry	marries	marrying	married

3
a beautiful
b greying
c driest
d worrying
e theories
f applying
g prettiest
h defying

4
a envying
b employing
c praying
d portraying

You be the teacher page 132

Correct structure: Working as a solo musician, Lennon composed well over one hundred songs. He was commended for his beautiful melodies and his enviable originality. The best-selling single of his solo career was 'Imagine', a song with a hopeful message for the future. Lennon proved he was more than just a Beatle—he was an artist.
Spelling errors: hopeful, more, beautiful, enviable, musician

UNIT 12 Narrative poems

Understanding the question page 135

1
- **a** alien: exotic, other, creature from outer space, monster, UFO, Martian
- **b** invasion: intrusion, assault, raid, breach
- **c** earth: globe, planet, sphere, dirt
- **d** narrative: anecdote, story, tale, legend, fable

2 create, write, construct

Language feature pages 139–143

1 **b** dark **c** lean **d** sparks **e** clattered **f** hugged

2 Answers could include:
b lovely **c** bad **d** wicked **e** lethal **f** annoying

3

a	a door closing	rumble
b	a cat	drip
c	an angry person	crash
d	a leaky tap	meow
e	a wave	squeak
f	a mouse	bellows
g	an empty stomach	bang

4 **a** squeaked **b** mumbled **c** groaning **d** swish **e** trickle **f** whooped

5
- **a** issued, spitless, lips
- **b** mellow, wedding, bells
- **c** strips, tinfoil, sinking

9 **a** form **b** me **c** fire **d** lights **e** snow

12
- **a** a big scary shark
- **b** 'like an ice vice'
- **c** The words 'dark deep' are used to draw our attention to the image of the sea.
- **d** 'heart lurches and groans'

Spotlight on spelling page 144

1 **b** lightning **c** chilli **d** prey **e** canvass **f** bored

2 **a** profit **b** breaking **c** lightening **d** lessen **e** sealing **f** bear

3 **a** see **b** passed **c** board **d** sense **e** paced **f** pain

You be the teacher page 145

Correct structure:
The lightning was a jagged rod of anger across the sky,
The thunder screamed in banging bursts away so high.
Staring up at that darkened and ominous Earthly ceiling,
I began to experience a most unusual and unearthly feeling.

Spelling errors: lightning, darkened, ceiling

Notes